Armies of the War of 1812

By

Gabriele Esposito

ARMIES OF THE WAR OF 1812
By Gabriele Esposito
Cover by Hugh Charles McBarron, Jr (Department of the Army)
This edition published in 2019

Winged Hussar Publishing, is an imprint of

Pike and Powder Publishing Group LLC
1525 Hulse Rd, Unit 1   1 Craven Lane, Box 66066
Point Pleasant, NJ 08742   Lawrence, NJ 08648-66066

Bibliographical References and Index
1. History. 2. United States. 3. War of 1812

Pike and Powder Publishing Group LLC All rights reserved
For more information on Pike and Powder Publishing Group, LLC,
visit us at www.PikeandPowder.com & www.wingedhussarpublishing.com

twitter: @pike_powder
facebook: @PikeandPowder

Table of Contents

Preface

This book is dedicated to my parents, Maria Rosaria and Benedetto, for their great love and precious support during the creative process of the present work. Special thanks are due to the editor of this volume, Vincent Rospond, for having enjoyed and sponsored this project since the early beginnings. Very special thanks goes to Olivier Millet, a great researcher of the War of 1812, for giving me permission to use the fantastic uniformologic plates that he has created on the armies of 1812-1815 in North America. His great generosity, typical of a real friend, has enabled me to illustrate the present title with hundreds of accurate and colourful reproductions of uniforms.

The colour plates reproduced in this book and created by Olivier are based on original models by Alexis Cabaret, which are available on the website: http://centjours.mont-saint-jean.com/; Olivier Millet, also, has a fantastic blog which displays most of his personal researches and color plates on the War of 1812: http://history-uniforms.over-blog.com/.

The main aim of this book is to present a detailed overview of the military forces involved into the War of 1812 - most of the text will be devoted to the organization of the opposing armies, which included troops of various kinds. For the British and Canadian forces, the analysis will focus on the years 1812-1815, while for the US Army the analysis will start from the disbanding of George Washington's Continental Army in 1783. This organization of the text is a specific choice of the author: understanding the military organization of the US Army during the War of 1812 is not possible without knowing which units made up the American military forces during the delicate period of 1783-1811. As a result of the above, the text will have the following structure on five chapters: the first one will deal with the history and organization of the US Army from the end of the Revolution to the outbreak of the new conflict with Britain; the second one will cover the US regular military forces during the crucial years of 1812-1815; the third chapter will be devoted to the various state militias of the USA, which played a very important role in defending the country from the British and native attacks; the fourth chapter will be dedicated to the British regular forces that garrisoned Canada during the conflict as well as to the military units that were sent as reinforcements by the Crown since 1812; the last chapter will cover with great detail the militia and volunteer units formed in the provinces of Canada (including the minor "Atlantic Colonies").

The text will try to show the importance of the militias in the War of 1812. Many people, in fact, think that the conflict was only fought among regular troops. In reality, both the US and the Canadian militiamen took part to the war in great numbers and were involved in many of the major battles. Finally, the text will have a final section devoted to the commentaries of the eight colour plates. This last part of the book will deal with the uniforms and weapons of the military forces described in the previous chapters. From a uniformology point of view, the War of 1812 was a very interesting conflict - it was contemporary to the Napoleonic Wars and saw the US regular army adopting new uniforms of clear British cut. The present book and its colour plates will give a lot of space also to the uniformology of the militias, which is generally little studied: in the USA the state militias used old-fashioned uniforms that generally followed the patterns of the former Continental Army. For Canada, in contrast, the militia uniforms were characterised by interesting local variations of the regular British military dress. For reasons of space, this text will not analyse the organization and uniforms of the US and British Navies; there will be some paragraphs, instead, devoted to the US Marines and Royal Marines (since these took part to several land battles during the conflict). It is important to remember, in addition, that the native American tribes were important participants to the War of 1812: these won't be covered in this book, but the select bibliography of the present text lists several titles devoted to their role in the conflict of 1812-1815.

Chronology

• November 7, 1811: Battle of Tippecanoe between US Army and Tecumseh's Confederacy. The natives, 700 warriors, are defeated by 1,000 American soldiers (regulars and militiamen).

• Early June, 1812: President James Madison presents a message to Congress in which he lists all the US complaints related to the usual British practice of "impressing" American sailors into the Royal Navy.

• June 18, 1812: US Congress declares war on Great Britain.

• June – August 1812: Riots break out in Baltimore and in some other cities of New England, in protest of the war.

• July 12, 1812: US military forces under General Hull launch the first invasion of Canada.

• July 17, 1812: British forces and their native allies start the besieging of the strategic Fort Mackinac in Michigan. The fort surrenders after a few hours of resistance.

• August 5, 1812: Battle of Brownstown in Michigan. Minor victory for Tecumseh and his British allies.

• August 16, 1812: General Hull surrenders the strategic Fort Detroit to the British forces without fighting. The first US invasion of Canada ends in complete disaster.

• August 19, 1812: During the first major naval clash of the war, the frigate USS Constitution defeats the frigate HMS Guerriere.

• October 13, 1812: Battle of Queenston Heights in Ontario. 1,300 British and Canadian soldiers are able to repel 3,550 US troops invading Canada from the Niagara Frontier.

• December 29, 1812: USS Constitution defeats HMS Java.

• January 18-23, 1813: Battle of Frenchtown in Michigan (also known as "River Raisin Massacre"). After some initial success, the US military forces operating in Michigan are defeated by the British troops and by Tecumseh's warriors. Around 100 American prisoners are massacred by the natives after the battle.

• February 22, 1813: Battle of Ogdensburg in New York. The British and Canadian forces eliminate any potential threat to their supply lines in the area of the Great Lakes.

• March 4, 1813: James Madison is inaugurated to his second term as President of the USA.

• April 27, 1813: Battle of York takes place during the second US invasion of Canada. The Americans are able to achieve their first significant victory of the war on land. York (present-day Toronto) is occupied by the US troops for six days. The shipyard, Government House and Parliament Buildings of the city are burned down.

• April – May, 1813: Siege of Fort Meigs in Ohio. 2,800 US defenders are able to repulse the assaults launched by 900 British/Canadian soldiers and 1,250 natives.

• September 10, 1813: Battle of Lake Erie in Ohio. Important US naval victory: American warships establish control over the waters of Lake Erie.

• October 5, 1813: Battle of the Thames between US Army and Tecumseh's Confederacy. Decisive American victory: Tecumseh is killed during the clash and the great native confederacy created by the warrior leader is dissolved.

• November 11, 1813: Battle of Crysler's Farm in Ontario. The US advance along the Saint Lawrence River is stopped by 900 British regulars and Canadian militiamen.

• April 4, 1814: In Europe Napoleon abdicates, thus leaving Great Britain free to concentrate all her military forces in North America against the USA.

• July 5, 1814: Battle of Chippawa in Ontario. Winfield Scott defeats the British/Canadian forces in a large pitched battle. For the first time, thanks to better training, the US troops are able to show all their great potential on the open field.

• July 22, 1814: The Treaty of Greenville is signed between several native tribes and the USA. Most of the tribes previously supporting Tecumseh decide to make peace with the US and thus form a new anti-British alliance with the Federal Government.

• July 25, 1814: Battle of Niagara Falls in Ontario. During the deadliest clash ever fought on Canadian territory, 2,500 Americans led by Winfield Scott are able to defeat 3,500 British/Canadian troops commanded by Gordon Drummond.

• August 24, 1814: Battle of Bladensburg in Maryland. During the so-called "Chesapeake Campaign" the British land an expeditionary force a few miles north of Washington. The US regulars and Maryland militiamen are soundly defeated; the Federal Capital of Washington is abandoned without fighting.

• August 25, 1814: The British Army occupies Washington. Most of the city is burned, including the White House and the Capitol. The British justify their action as a retaliation for the American destruction of York.

• August 27, 1814: Fort Warburton, also known as Fort Washington, is abandoned without fighting by the US Army and is destroyed in order to prevent its capture from the British.

• August – September, 1814: The British launch a successful raid against Alexandria, in Virginia. The Potomac River is controlled by the Royal Navy.

• September 11, 1814: Battle of Lake Champlain in New York. The British invasion of New England is stopped by the US regulars and militiamen. 9,000 British troops are decisively defeated by 6,000 Americans.

• September 12, 1814: Battle of North Point in Maryland. A British landing force of 4,000 soldiers is defeated by 3,000 Maryland militiamen.

• September, 1814: Battle of Baltimore in Maryland. Fort McHenry is heavily bombarded by the Royal Navy, but the American defenders of the city are able to repulse the enemy assault and to cause heavy casualties to the British. The bombardment of Fort McHenry inspired Francis Scott Key to compose the poem "Defence of Fort McHenry" that later became the lyrics for "The Star-Spangled Banner" (the national anthem of the USA).

• November 6, 1814: Battle of Malcolm's Mills in Ontario. Victorious American raids across the Ontario Peninsula led to the subsequent reconquest of Fort Detroit.

• November, 1814: Battle of Pensacola in western Florida. Andrew Jackson expels the British troops stationed in the region.

• December 24, 1814: Signing of the Treaty of Ghent between the USA and Great Britain brings the War of 1812 to an end. The balance of power in North America is brought back to the status quo. The troops on the field, however, are not informed of the treaty for several weeks and thus military operations continue.

• January 8, 1815: Battle of New Orleans in Louisiana. 5,700 US troops under command of Andrew Jackson defeat a British expeditionary corps of 8,000 regulars. The British invasion of Louisiana is repulsed; the greatest American victory in the war causes severe losses to the British Army.

• February 16, 1815: The Treaty of Ghent is ratified by the Congress and President Madison declares the end of the hostilities with Great Britain.

Chapter 1: The US Army From 1783 to 1811

After the end of the American Revolution, the great Continental Army created and forged under George Washington was disbanded by the Congress. The Treaty of Paris, bringing the war between Great Britain and the USA to an end, was signed on 3 September 1783: by that time the American Army was camped along the Hudson River at New Windsor, after having terminated the siege operations against Yorktown. It comprised approximately 7,000 - 8,000 men, all veterans who had served their young nation with great courage. By the end of the war, however, many of these soldiers were ill-clad and underfed: they lacked adequate supplies and had not been paid for a long time. The difficulties of a terrible war had caused serious problems to the economy of the new nation and the USA was no longer in conditions nor had the desire to maintain a large military force of regulars. With the defeat of the British, it was now time to demobilize the Continental Army and thus cut the military costs in a significant way. On 24 September 1783, shortly after the signing of the Paris Treaty, the Congress formally ordered Washington to demobilize the Continental Army. The demobilization order was not too strict: Washington, in fact, was free to decide how many soldiers should remain under arms. The great general waited for some time, until the last British troops abandoned New York, before reorganizing the US Army. According to the new structure in place in 1783, the latter was an amalgamation of just 600 men: one regiment of infantry with two attached companies of artillery. The new infantry unit was known as "1st American Regiment" or as "Jackson's Continental Regiment", since it was commanded by Colonel Henry Jackson. From a formal point of view, the Continental Army was not disbanded and thus now corresponded to this single regiment (this being the reason why it had the adjective "Continental" in its name). This unit lasted until 3 June 1784: on that date a new "1st American Regiment" was formally established, which was theoretically organized on nine companies; during those same days, all the other units of the Continental Army were disbanded. Most of the soldiers who made up the new regiment were veterans coming from the Massachusetts infantry regiments. The senior artillery company came from "Lamb's Continental Artillery Regiment" (an elite unit of the Continental Army, which had been structured on 10 companies until demobilization); the junior one was raised in Pennsylvania. Obviously 500 infantrymen and 100 artillerymen were not enough to defend the boundaries of the new nation, but the Congress and the majority of the Americans were not in favour of a large permanent force in keeping with the revolutionary ideals.

Some American leaders recognized the necessity of building up a new army, to be used in time of peace. These had different opinions about the quantity and quality of the troops that should be kept in service. Arsenals and other important military sites had to be adequately garrisoned; in addition, the forts of the western frontier had to be defended from collisions between natives and Americans pushing the western frontier (which also continued after peace was made with Britain). At this time, the former colonies were united under the Articles of Confederation which placed more power in the hands of individual states. Some members of the Congress were strongly against the existence of any regular standing army: according to their view, each state could defend itself using militia forces, which had been the main component of the American military during the long Colonial Period. Professional armies had a high cost and there were limited ways for the Congress at that time to raise funds; in addition, a regular military force was viewed to potentially represent a serious menace to the republican freedom of the new nation. During the Revolution, states raised their own regiments and together with local militias had showed their potential on several occasions – albeit after a long period of training. There were other American political leaders who had different opinions: these, led by George Washington, were strongly convinced that a regular military force – albeit small – was absolutely needed. While this debate was still in process, the disbandment of the Continental Army caused some additional problems: officers and soldiers of some units were not paid in some time and feared that after the demobilization of their corps they would never be paid. As a result, petitions and agitation became very common: these events, together with a riot in Philadelphia, had a negative impact on many members of the Congress. The politicians feared a large-scale mutiny of the troops and saw them as a menace to the internal stability of the country. Thanks to the steady hand of their old commander nothing serious happened and the demobilization was completed in a safe way.

States and Territories of the United States of America
June 4 1812 to December 11 1816

Map of the United States during the War of 1812 (Wikipedia)

The riots of Philadelphia and the strong protests of the army's officers, however, had a great impact over the American public opinion and led to a drastic decision from the Congress. On 2 June 1784, it ordered General Knox (senior officer of the US Army) to disband the "1st American Regiment". In total, only 80 regular soldiers were to remain on active service: these were to guard military stores at West Point and Fort Pitt, thus having only garrison roles. These few remaining regulars were part of the senior artillery company commanded by Major Doughty. No officer above the rank of captain was to remain in service, since members of the Congress were convinced that officers had been the real planners of the riots that occurred during previous months. On 3 June 1784, just one day after the disbandment of the "1st American Regiment", the Congress ordered the recruitment of ten new companies (eight of infantry and two of artillery) from the militias of the following states: Pennsylvania, Connecticut, New York and New Jersey. These were assembled into a single unit simply known as the "Regiment of Infantry" (also known, again, as the "1st American Regiment"), which was not a regular corps but a sort of "federal militia" formed with contingents of various states. The new unit was to serve for just one year, thus having a temporary nature; in total, it comprised 700 men. It was the result of a compromise, between the need for some standing military force and the fears of the Congress (that did not want the reestablishment of a regular army). Meanwhile, the situation on the borders was not quiet: the British and the native Americans were still active in the Ohio Valley and Great Lakes areas, while the Spaniards in Florida and Louisiana were quite aggressive in their border policy. The new recruits were soon scattered across the borders of the USA, being stationed in the northern areas of New York State (to guard the area of the Great Lakes from British incursions) and in the newly-conquered territories located west of the Appalachian Mountains. The various detachments of the regiment were garrisoned in isolated outposts and consisted of just a few soldiers under command of a junior officer. In April 1785, when the period of service of the "Regiment of Infantry" was about to expire, the Congress made a call for another 700 recruits; this time, however, the new soldiers were to serve for a period of three years. In addition, they were not to be detached from the state militias but to enlist directly into federal service. After just one year during which it was a "hybrid" military force, the US Army was again formed by a proper regular unit.

The years following the American Revolution were characterised by economic depression, which caused some civilian unrest. Fearing that the outbreak of a popular revolt could have had terrible consequences on the development of the new nation, the Congress finally understood that regular military units were necessary not only for foreign policy but also to secure internal stability. In 1786-87 Massachusetts was rocked by the uprising known as "Shay's Rebellion", which caused trouble for the central government. Lacking a sufficient number of troops to quell the revolt, in October 1786 the Congress ordered the recruitment of further regular soldiers from those states that had not contributed to the formation of the "Regiment of Infantry". The states of New Hampshire, Massachusetts, Rhode Island, Connecticut, Maryland and Virginia had to raise a total of 1,340 men; to serve for a period of three years, with the main objective of suppressing the revolt in Massachusetts. The recruiting operations went on very slowly, to the point that the rebellion was over before the new corps was formed thanks to funds raised privately in Massachusetts for a local force. Since "Shay's Rebellion" was over, Congress decided to disband the newly-formed units except for two companies of artillery (that were employed to guard the Springfield Arsenal and West Point).

In October 1787 the Congress renewed the authorization for 700 men of the "1st American Regiment", which was now to comprise eight infantry companies plus four attached artillery companies. In that period the traditional division between Federalist and Anti-Federalist members of the Congress became extremely apparent during the Constitutional Convention of Philadelphia: the question regarding the new military asset of the USA was one of the most discussed, which neither side was willing to give in. On 21 June 1788 the Convention of Philadelphia promulgated a new Constitution, and this had important effects over the military. According to the new constitutional system, the central government was directly responsible for raising and maintaining a regular army: all the federal military expenses were to be paid by the various states, since the Congress now had the power to impose and collect taxes. The President was the commander-in-chief of the US Army and the choice of maintaining a regular military force was to be reviewed every two years by the same Congress. The various states continued to have complete control over the appointment of officers and training for the militia, but the latter could be organized and disciplined by the central government in case of military emergency (like a foreign invasion). The structure of the army remained the same: a single infantry regiment having eight companies with four attached artillery companies (in 1789 these were assembled into a single artillery battalion). Soldiers continued to serve for periods of three years, being mostly located in the various forts of the Ohio River Valley. In 1790 the Congress authorized a little expansion of the regular army, with the formation of another four infantry companies that were added to the single regiment (which was now to have three battalions with four companies each).

At the beginning of the new decade thousands of colonists started to move west, crossing the Appalachian Mountains and settle in new fertile territories. These settlers needed the protection of the army, since the territories that they wanted to occupy were mostly inhabited by hostile native tribes. This was particularly true for the Ohio area, where the natives were supported by the British authorities of Canada. The Crown still controlled some key points in Ohio, which had not been abandoned after the peace of 1783; the British, however, were just done fighting against the Americans and thus could not start a new conflict against the USA. As a result, since the native Americans of Ohio were quite numerous, the British preferred arming and supporting the natives in their struggle against the United States instead of being directly involved into the military operations. The natives were convinced that the boundary between their territories and those of the USA was marked by the Ohio River; the Americans, instead, claimed that the whole territory of Ohio had been ceded to them according to the peace treaty of 1783 (the tribes of the region had all fought on the side of Great Britain). Due to these contrasting views of the question, war between the USA and the Ohio tribes became inevitable. The latter included some powerful tribes, which had significant resources from a military point of view. After a rapid escalation of violence, during which the US Army tried to preserve peace, full scale war broke out in Ohio between the colonists and the native Americans. As a result, in 1790, President George Washington was obliged to send part of the regular army in a punitive expedition against the natives. Due to logistical problems and the scarce discipline of the soldiers, the expedition was a complete failure for the US troops. In 1791 they mounted a new offensive against the native confederation in Ohio and Congress authorized the formation of a second regiment of infantry (3 March). The latter was to have the same structure of the existing one, with three battalions of four companies each. In addition, Congress also authorized recruiting another 2,000 soldiers who were known as "Levies" - these were militiamen who had to serve temporarily under federal officers, until the end of the new war against the local tribes. On 3 November 1791 an American military force of 1,400 regulars, levies and militiamen was defeated at the Battle of Wabash: in total 600 Americans were killed and 300 wounded, in the worst defeat ever suffered by the US Army on its national territory.

After the disaster of Wabash, it became clear that the United States badly needed a proper army, since the natives of the Ohio had proved to be a very strong enemy. The American Army had no cavalry unit since 1783 and this caused serious troubles during the unlucky campaigns of 1790 and 1791. As a result, in 1792, the Congress decided that the time had come to completely reorganize the US military forces. Another three regiments of infantry (with three battalions each) and one squadron of dragoons (of four troops) were formed, but this was just an initial measure. Under personal supervision from President Washington, Knox and Baron von Steuben the American military forces were then re-structured as the "Legion of the United States". At that time the term "legion" was particularly popular in the military world and was used to indicate independent corps that comprised different branches of service (typically infantry, cavalry and artillery). This was also the case of the "Legion of the United States", which was authorised by Congress on 27 December 1792 and comprised the following units: four "Sub-Legions" each with three battalions of infantry, one battalion of rifles, one troop of dragoons and one company of artillery. Each "Sub-Legion" could operate as an independent "small army", since it comprised units from all the branches of service. The whole Legion was under command of Major General Anthony Wayne.

The infantry battalions, 12 in total, continued to be structured on four companies each; the Battalions of Rifles, a new formation, were elite light infantry units that comprised four companies each. The four troops of dragoons had been originally assembled into a single squadron but now were assigned to each "Sub-Legion"; it is important to remember that the members of these mounted corps were light dragoons and not heavy ones, since cavalry in North America had always been lightly-equipped from the days of the British colonial rule. All four companies of artillery already existed before 1792, but from this moment there was no more distinction among them between "field" and "garrison" units. In total the "Legion of the United States" comprised 5,000 soldiers, who were much better trained and disciplined than previously. Clothing, rations, pay and morale were all improved; Wayne took all the time that was necessary to prepare the new American military force and this period of intensive training had many positive results.

On 9 May 1794 a new "Corps of Artillerists and Engineers" was formed, with four artillery battalions of four companies each; the latter were mostly stationed along the coastal areas, in order to protect them from potential British naval raids while the main army was fighting against the native Americans. On 30 June of the same year, Wayne and his new military forces crushed the Ohio tribes at the decisive Battle of Fallen Timbers. After some difficult years, the US Army had been able to regain its previous glory: on 3 August 1795 the Treaty of Greenville brought the war on the frontier to an end, with the native Americans renouncing to most of their lands located in modern Ohio and eastern Indiana. During 1794 the militias played an important military role, since while the regular army was fighting against the natives another popular revolt broke out inside the USA. The latter, known as "Whiskey Rebellion", which was crushed with little bloodshed by the state militias (which were guided by General Washington during the last phase of the campaign).

General Anthony Wayne (Wikipedia)

After the Treaty of Greenville, members of the Congress started to think that a large standing army was no longer needed. They maintained that the "Legion of the United States" professionalism had a high cost and thus it was soon decided to reorganize the American military forces again. From 31 October 1796, according to the new structure, the US Army was to comprise the following units: four regiments of infantry (each on 8 companies), two troops of light dragoons and the "Corps of Artillerists and Engineers". At this time Europe was ravaged by the terrible wars that followed the outbreak of the French Revolution. The United States tried to remain out of these conflicts, but the signing of a "Treaty of Amity" with Great Britain in 1795 led to serious diplomatic tensions with France. The new republican government of that country, in fact, considered the new peaceful relations between the USA and Great Britain as a political menace. As a result, incidents between American commercial vessels and French warships became quite common. In addition, the French also instigated and supported the native tribes of the southwest in their struggle against the American colonists. This period of tension lasted for five years until 1800 and is commonly known as "Quasi-War", because the situation arrived very near to the outbreak of real hostilities. Due to the new naval menace represented by France, the Congress ordered the formation of a new "Regiment of Artillerists and Engineers" on 27 April 1798. The latter had three battalions of four companies each and was used to garrison the forts and ports located on the Atlantic coastline. During the following months the possibility of a large-

THE US LINE INFANTRY IN 1812

Captain Drummer   **Soldiers**   **Corporal Sergeant**

THE UNIFORMS OF THE US LINE INFANTRY, 1812

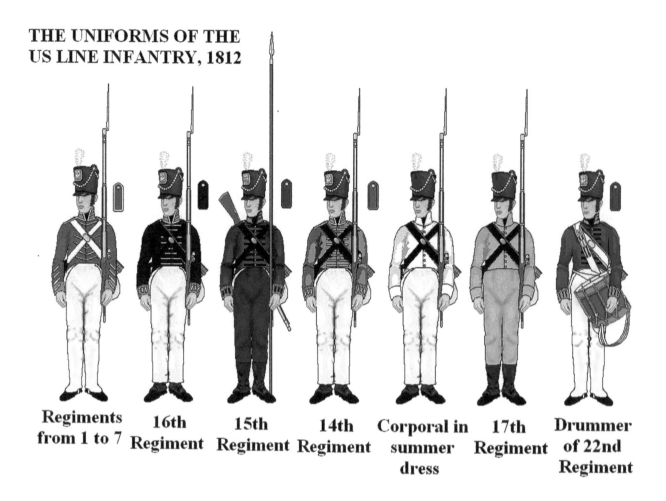

| Regiments from 1 to 7 | 16th Regiment | 15th Regiment | 14th Regiment | Corporal in summer dress | 17th Regiment | Drummer of 22nd Regiment |

scale conflict with France became very real; as a result, Congress authorized the formation of the following new military units (16 July 1798): 12 regiments of infantry (having same structure of the existing ones) and 1 regiment of light dragoons (with eight troops, including the two ones already in existence). When the "Quasi-War" came to an end and a new treaty was signed with France in 1800, the general structure of the US Army saw another demobilization. On 14 May 1800 the organization of the American military forces was laid out as follows: four regiments of infantry, two troops of dragoons and two regiments of artillery. The only unit formed during the "Quasi-War" to be retained was the "Regiment of Artillerists and Engineers", which had been enlarged with the addition of another battalion since 3 March 1799. On that same day the "Corps of Artillerists and Engineers" was renamed as "1st Regiment of Artillerists and Engineers" and the "Regiment of Artillerists and Engineers" was renamed as "2nd Regiment of Artillerists and Engineers".

In 1801 Thomas Jefferson became the new President of the United States; this event had significant consequences for the history of the US Army, in contrast to John Adams, Jefferson was strongly convinced that the country did not need a large military force made up of regulars. The real defenders of the new nation would have to be the militiamen, as it had always been since the early decades of the 17th century. Jefferson, however, was well aware that at least a small corps of regulars was needed: in his view, they only had to perform defensive duties of a static nature (like garrisoning of frontier forts). After all the political situation had changed from the previous decades and now America was not directly menaced by any European power. As a result of all the above, President Jefferson completely reorganized the army and reduced its general numbers in 1802. On 16 March 1802 the Congress fixed the following "Military Peace Establishment" for the US Army: two regiments of infantry (each with 10 companies), one regiment of artillery (on 5 battalions, each with 4 companies) and one corps of engineers (made up of just 20 specialist officers and cadets). In addition, the Academy at West Point was created. Jefferson and his military advisors had the clear intention of transforming the little regular army into a highly professional military force. To achieve this however, the officer corps needed to be trained in a modern military school, where the latest military innovations coming from Europe could be studied. During previous decades, the US Army had suffered from a chronic lack of officers with good technical competences; this was particularly true for what regarded military engineering and artillery. As a result, Jefferson did his best to set up a military academy that could give to its cadets a solid scientific background. Jefferson had the intention of using the army as an element that could improve the infrastructure of the nation and thus its officers needed to have the same personal preparation as a civilian specialist. Thus, West Point graduated engineers who were also officers. The only alternative to this policy would have been that of recruiting specialist officers from foreign nations, but these men would have never been as loyal as real American officers. By the outbreak of the 1812 War with Britain, however, only 89 officers had completed their military instruction at West Point. The new establishment of the army comprised no cavalry or rifles units, since Jefferson was strongly convinced that these would have been provided by the state militias in case of need. Regarding the artillery, it is important to note that the two former units of artillerymen lost their engineer component and were assembled into a single corps known as "Regiment of Artillerists". During the period 1784-1802, the US Marine Corps more or less had the same destiny of the other regular military units being contracted and expanded as necessary. After the surrender of the British, in April 1783, both the Continental Navy and the Continental Marines were disbanded. The latter were reformed on 11 July 1798, in view of the imminent war against France (during the "Quasi-War" period, which saw also the re-creation of the US Navy on 27 March 1794). The new Marine Corps was to consist of a single battalion with 500 naval infantrymen; despite being a very young military unit, it soon distinguished itself during the First Barbary War of 1801-1805.

On 4 July 1803 the United States greatly enlarged their territory by purchasing the vast region of Louisiana from France. Until the end of the Seven Year's War Louisiana had been a French colony, but in 1762 the defeated French were obliged to cede it to Britain and Spain. The areas of Louisiana located west of the Mississippi River were annexed to the Spanish colonies, while those located to the east were occupied by Britain. With the independence of the United States, the eastern section of Louisiana became part of the new nation; this was still mostly unexplored and inhabited only by natives. In 1800, while Napoleon was First Consul of France, a new treaty of alliance was concluded between the French and the Spaniards in order to fight against Britain. A0ccording to this Treaty of San Ildefonso the western part of Louisiana was to be transferred from Spain to France. Napoleon, however, had no enough military resources in the American continent to defend Louisiana in an effective way from British attacks. Since his national economy needed money in order to finance the continuous wars against other European powers, Napoleon decided that probably the best decision for the future of Louisiana was that of selling the whole territory to the United States. The Americans had showed interest in acquiring this area and thus the "Louisiana Purchase" became reality. France ceded the region,

including the important city of New Orleans, for a mere 50 million francs (11 million dollars) and cancellation of previous debts contracted with the United States. As a result, without firing a single shot, the Americans enlarged their national territory with 828,000 square miles of fertile land located west of the Mississippi (which had marked the western border of the nation since 1783). The annexation of such a vast territory had important consequences for the US military: an adequate defence of Louisiana was something very difficult to achieve, due to the small number of regulars available. In addition, the native tribes of the region were particularly numerous and hostile towards encroaching settlers. Despite all these difficulties, the US Army had a decisive role in exploring the Louisiana territory and building the first few government structures there.

Thomas Jefferson, third President of the United States (Rembrandt Peale, 1800, Wikipedia)

During those same years the regular army was involved with the "Lewis and Clark Expedition", which was organized by Jefferson in order to map the newly-purchased territory of Louisiana. Lewis and Clark had to find a practical land route across the western half of Northern America, in order to establish a first US presence in regions that could be easily claimed by European powers like Britain or Spain. In view of the expedition, a special "task force" was detached from the US Army under command of Lewis and Clark: this was called "Corps of Discovery" and was formed with volunteers who underwent a special training before starting their mission. The expedition lasted for two years and four months, covering 7,689 miles. Initially there were 34 soldiers, which was later reduced to 26. While this and other explorations took place, the bulk of the US Army took possession of Louisiana and placed garrisons at the key locations of the region. A total of 400 men were sent to New Orleans: these consisted of six artillery companies and four infantry companies (the infantry from the "2nd Regiment of Infantry"). The exact border between American Louisiana and Spanish Mexico was not extremely clear at the time and the Spaniards had all the needed military resources to mount potential invasion directed against New Orleans. This international situation was one of the main reasons behind the strong military presence of the US in Louisiana. Border tensions with Spain continued to escalate for some time, until most of the existing questions were settled. By 1805, however, the USA started to be menaced again by their old British enemies and this led to a gradual but significant change in Jefferson's foreign policy. During the summer of 1807 a serious international incident involved some US and British warships in waters off the coast of Virginia; this event, known as "Chesapeake Affair", renewed the traditional naval rivalry existing between the Americans and the British for control of North Atlantic. President Jefferson was strongly convinced that the outbreak of war was imminent and thus urged the expansion of US armed forces. During the years before 1808 he had tried to modernize the state militias by improving their training, but most of his efforts in this sense came to nothing.

On 12 April 1808 the Congress authorized the following new structure for the army: seven regiments of infantry (each with 10 companies), one regiment of rifles (on 10 companies), one regiment of light dragoons (with 8 troops), one regiment of artillery (on 5 battalions, each with 4 companies), one regiment of light artillery (on 10 companies) and one corps of engineers (which kept its previous establishment). The idea behind the creation of a light artillery regiment development of horse batteries, which could move very rapidly and thus support the other units of the army where needed. The "Regiment of Light Artillery", in fact, was a unit of mounted artillery (except for its first company, which consisted of field guns and became mounted only in 1812). The new regiment of rifles was to have a very important tactical role: to operate across a large section of the country covered with woods, like those of North America, a conventional line infantry contingent needed to have a good number of light infantry skirmishers who could cover its flanks and act as scouts. In addition, the rifle-men were the perfect soldiers to be employed in military operations conducted against the native population in broken terrain. Mobility and speed were key elements in the North American warfare which could determine the success or the failure of an entire operation. Finally, the rifles had another great advantage over the line infantry: being armed with rifled guns, they were trained as experienced marksmen capable of hitting targets over a greater distance. The mythology of the American militiaman was as a "rifleman" that did not bear out in practice. When it was properly carried out, however, this had extremely important tactical consequences during the Revolution against Britain; on several occasions, in fact, the line infantry "redcoats" of the enemy were ambushed and defeated thanks to the superior mobility of the American "minutemen" (who could assemble their forces and move in a few minutes).

James Madison, fourth President of the United States

(Gilbert Stuart, 1829, Wikipedia)

On 4 March 1809, after Jefferson's two terms, James Madison became the new President of the United States. The situation with Britain was still very tense on the Atlantic, since British war-ships continued to stop and inspect any American vessel in search of sailors who had deserted from the Royal Navy. During those years Britain was blocking most of the European coastline, in order to stop any foreign nation could trade with France to defeat Napoleon. American ships were formally neutral, but British authorities had little respect of this and continued to stop them for strict controls. Sometimes the Americans refused to be inspected and incidents like the "Chesapeake Affair" occurred. Meanwhile, the relations with the powerful native tribes of the North-East started to deteriorate again: a new native leader, Tecumseh, began to form a confederation of different tribal groups in order to defend the native territory from American expansionism. In doing this he was strongly supported by his brother, who was an important religious leader commonly known as the "Prophet". Tecumseh and his brother even built a large settlement called "Prophetstown", where all the followers of the "Prophet" lived with their families. After some years of inactivity, the US government understood that Tecumseh was a potential menace for the stability of the frontier: he was a great military leader and could count on the indirect British support coming from Canada. By 1810 native raids against American settlements became increasingly frequent and thus the regular army had to intervene in order to protect the homesteaders. Madison feared that America would not be able to fight against the natives and against Britain at the same time; as a result, he ordered to his generals to attack and defeat Tecumseh as soon as possible. In November 1811 the US Army, under command of Gov. William H. Harrison, arrived at Prophetstown while Tecumseh was away. The ensuing Battle of Tippecanoe saw the American troops defending their camp from enemy attacks and causing heavy losses to the natives; after the clash the inhabitants of Prophetstown abandoned their settlement and the latter was burned by Harrison. The natives had been defeated, but they were still able to fight; during the War of 1812, as an ally of Britain, Tecumseh continued his resistance against the Americans and the settlement of Prophetstown was rebuilt. On 18 June 1812 the war between USA and Britain began: a new page in the history of the US Army was going to be written.

THE US FOOT ARTILLERY, 1810

Captain Drummer   **Soldiers**   **Corporal Sergeant**

Chapter 2: The Organization of the US Army From 1812 to 1815

When the war with Britain started, the US were absolutely unprepared for a large-scale conflict with a great European power. The regular army was quite small and had very little experience with conventional warfare: the potential military resources of the country were great, but these needed time and money to be fully mobilized. Despite all the above, the "War Hawks" of the Congress were able to convince President Madison that the US needed to respond to perceived British infractions and war was finally declared. Many American politicians had great expansionist ambitions and were sure that Canada could be easily conquered with a few weeks of campaign. In their opinion the large British colonies of North America were garrisoned by too few troops in order to be defended; in addition, most of them hoped that the Canadians would revolt against the British in order to achieve independence from the Crown. Reality was very far from the optimistic expectations of the "War Hawks". Despite being at war with Napoleon in Europe, the British had enough soldiers in Canada to fight against the US. In contrast to American expectations the Canadians, remained loyal to the Crown and defended their territory with all the resources they had. Even the French settlers, who had not accepted the British conquest of Canada from France at the end of the Seven Years' War, gave their loyal contribution to the British cause. At sea the general situation was a bit different, since the Americans had gradually rebuilt their Navy and transformed it into an efficient force - the US frigates and their crews were second to none and could fight against the warships of the Royal Navy on almost equal terms. In addition, the British were fighting on all the seas of the globe against the French and thus could not deploy large naval squadrons against the Americans. This meant that the US Navy could count on a local numerical superiority at times even though they had no capital ships, which would have important consequences during the conflict. Because of the rational for the war and the stakes against this enemy, some historians have called this conflict the "Second War of American Independence". In view of the potential war against Britain, the US Army started to be expanded from January 1812; several months before the official declaration of war. Several new units were formed, creating the following general structure by early June 1812: 17 regiments of line infantry, 1 regiment of rifles, 2 regiments of light dragoons, 3 regiments of foot artillery, 1 regiment of light (horse) artillery, 1 corps of engineers, 1 corps of artificers, 1 company of bombardiers/sappers/miners and 6 independent companies of mounted "Rangers".

The Line Infantry

The seventeen line infantry regiments existing by early June 1812 were all organized on two battalions, each having five companies. Differing from most armies of the time, the various companies were not distinguished between "centre" ones of fusiliers and "flank" ones of grenadiers or chasseurs - all American line infantrymen were fusiliers. On 26 June 1812, just a few days after the declaration of war, the Congress ordered the formation of another eight infantry regiments (thus bringing the total to 25); at the same time, the internal organization of all the line infantry regiments was changed. According to the new structure, all the 25 infantry units were to consist of single battalions with ten companies: they retained their designation of "regiments" and their previous numerical establishment, but their new organization with just one battalion was much more flexible than the previous one. On paper, each line infantry company comprised the following: one captain, one lieutenant, one sub-lieutenant, one ensign, four sergeants, four corporals, two drummers and one hundred soldiers (for a total of 116 men). Generally speaking, however, the infantry regiments rarely reached their formal establishment of over 1,000 men and generally had only 600 soldiers (more or less being the equivalent of a standard European infantry battalion). On 29 January 1813, after understanding that the war would have continued for long time, the Congress ordered the formation of another twenty-one line infantry regiments (bringing the total to 46). During the Niagara Campaign of 1814 a special infantry brigade was formed by assembling four regiments (the 9th, 11th, 22nd and 25th), which were put under command of General Winfield Scott. Soon after its formation the brigade was sent to a training camp located near the Niagara frontier, where its infantrymen underwent intensive training under personal control of Scott. The latter, albeit being very young, did his best to improve the discipline and tactical organization of his men. At that time the US Army did not have a standardized drill for the infantry, with several foreign military manuals being employed by officers to train their rankers. As a result, there was a lot of confusion among the various units and the training taught to the regiments varied a lot in terms of quality. Scott decided to follow one of the best drill manuals of the time, which was written for the French infantry in 1791. Thanks to this choice, the four regiments of his brigade soon became the best foot units of the US Army. When training was completed, "Scott's Brigade" was able to advance and fire in perfect close order as the best British infantry formations; the results of this fundamental change became apparent during the Battle of Chippewa, which saw the US infantry perform perfect manoeuvres under intense enemy fire. "Scott's Brigade" had a significant peculiarity regarding the organization of the units: each company of its four regiments, in fact, had to provide one sapper. Since each regiment had ten companies, there were ten sappers for each regiment who formed a pioneer squad (commanded by a corporal). The presence of pioneers who could "open the way" enabled the units of the "Scott's Brigade" to move rapidly on each kind of terrain, even the densely forested areas. On 3 March 1815, just a few weeks after the end of the war with Britain, the total number of line infantry regiments was reduced from forty-six to a peace time establishment of just eight.

Gen. Winfield Scott, an engraving from the 1840's
(Wikipedia)

THE US LINE
INFANTRY FROM 1813

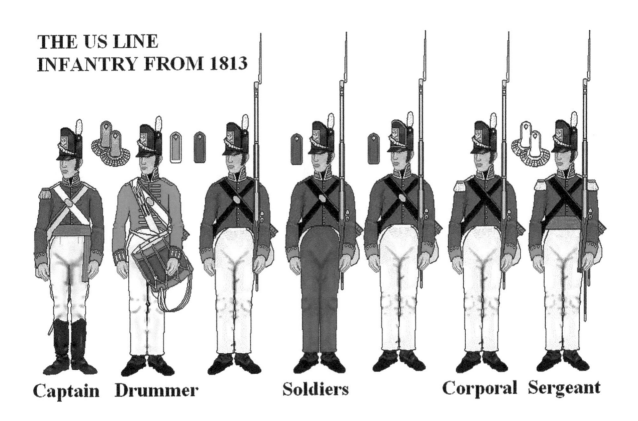

Captain Drummer   Soldiers   Corporal Sergeant

THE US LINE INFANTRY FROM 1813

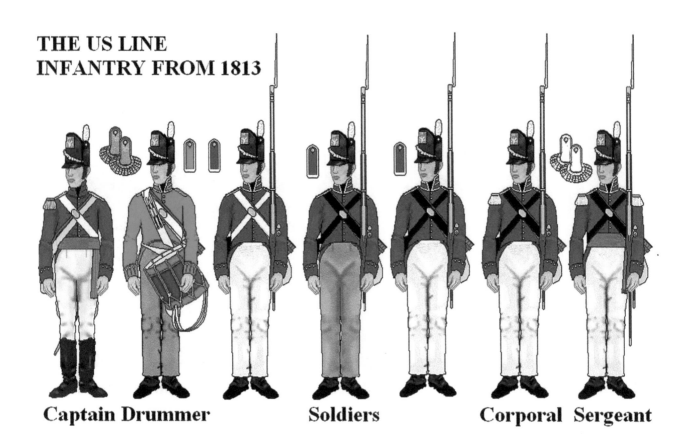

Captain   Drummer   Soldiers   Corporal Sergeant

SCOTT'S BRIGADE, 1814

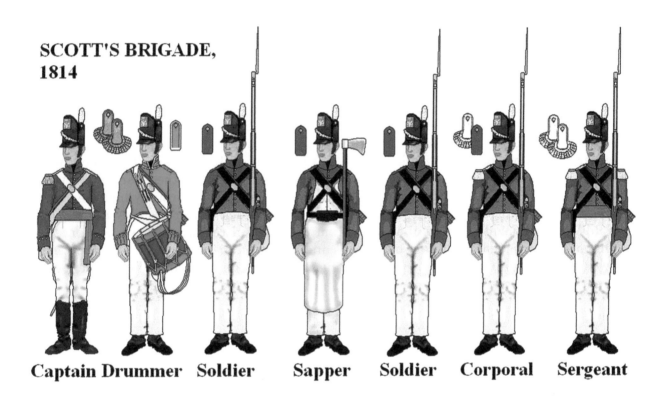

Captain **Drummer** **Soldier** **Sapper** **Soldier** **Corporal** **Sergeant**

The Rifles

The riflemen were considered as an elite unit inside the US Army, since their light infantry role and rifled carbines made them perfectly suited for warfare on rough terrain. During the period between 1783 and 1811, American infantry mostly fought against the native tribes and thus had abandoned the tactical doctrine to manoeuvre in close order as the European line infantry of the time usually did. After fighting against the British regular infantry during the first battles of the war, the Americans understood that their line infantry had to train in close order in order to have some chance of victory against the British: only the proper "rifle" units were to act as light infantrymen, while the rest of the foot troops were to manoeuvre in a European way. An American on the frontier, because of his lifestyle, had a great potential as a light infantryman. Initially, when the war broke out, the US Army comprised just one "Regiment of Riflemen": this had two battalions with five companies each like the line infantry units, but the number of men in each company was just 86 instead of 116. The ten companies were recruited from different areas of the US: three in New York and Vermont; three in the Louisiana and Mississippi Territories; four in Ohio, Kentucky and Indiana Territory. Many of the soldiers came from frontier regions where all settlers were experienced marksmen. During the early months of the war the "Regiment of Riflemen" performed extremely well against the British, especially in conducting "irregular" operations on the Canadian border. As a result, on 10 February 1814 the Congress decided to raise another three regiments of rifles. Due to this measure, the existing unit became known as the "1st Regiment of Riflemen". The three new regiments formally had the same internal structure of the existing one, but due to the general lack of recruits they never reached their full establishments. Differentiating it from the original regiment, these new ones were not employed during major military operations and remained in garrison in the outposts of the vast western frontier. On 17 May 1815, following the end of the war with Britain, the four rifle regiments were consolidated into a single "Regiment of Riflemen".

THE US REGIMENT OF RIFLES

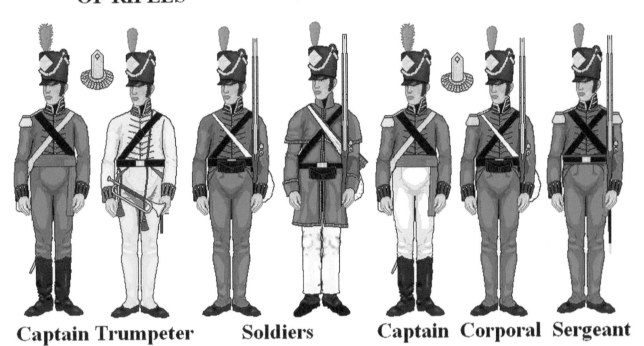

Captain   Trumpeter   Soldiers   Captain   Corporal   Sergeant

The Light Dragoons

The light dragoons of the US Army had a tradition that dated back to the times of the Revolution. During the long war against the Thirteen Colonies, in fact, the British employed mostly light dragoons against the rebels and not heavy units. As a result, the cavalry of George Washington's Continental Army was modelled on the light horse units deployed by the enemy. For many reasons the choice of employing only light cavalry in North America was a realistic one: the terrain, in fact, was too vast and too broken to permit an effective use of regular horsemen with heavy equipment. The US cavalry primarily acted as a reconnaissance force, since the environmental conditions of North America rarely permitted the use of cavalry for traditional charges on open terrain. The "Regiment of Light Dragoons" already existing in January 1812 had been formed on 12 April 1808: it had eight troops and was not completely mounted (the dismounted troops acting as light infantry). On 11 January 1812, during the pre-war mobilization, a second regiment of light dragoons was created and thus the existing one was re-named as "1st Regiment of Light Dragoons". The two cavalry units were never used as consolidated regiments during the war, since their various troops were usually attached to different contingents of the army that operated independently. The few light dragoons attached to each military formation were employed as scouts, escorts and couriers: they never performed as "shock" cavalry. On 30 March 1814, due to the scarcity of new recruits and of suitable mounts, the two regiments of light dragoons were consolidated as a single unit (always with eight troops). In 1815 this "Regiment of Light Dragoons" was finally disbanded as part of that year's demobilization.

US LIGHT DRAGOONS
1812 - 1815

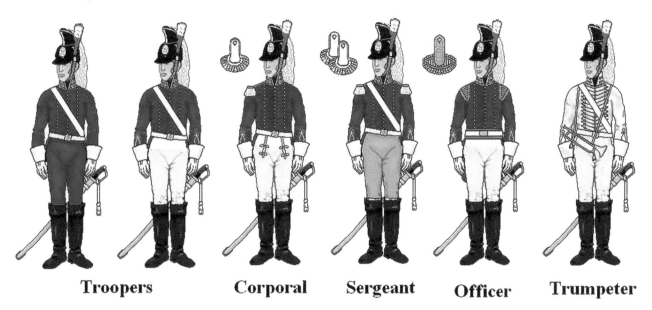

Troopers   **Corporal**   **Sergeant**   **Officer**   **Trumpeter**

The Foot Artillery and Light Artillery

Before 1812 the US Army contained just one regiment of foot artillery, which had 20 companies in four battalions (each of the latter comprising 4 companies). During the war mobilization, on 11 January 1812, another two regiments were created having the same structure of the existing one. In practice, however, the two new units never reached their full establishment and thus the whole US foot artillery never had the 60 planned companies. After creation of the new regiments the original one, which was known as "Regiment of Artillerists", was re-named as "1st Regiment of Artillery". Similar to what happened for the light dragoons, the artillery regiments were rarely employed as consolidated units: their companies, in fact, were attached to the various military formations in order to operate the field batteries of the latter. In addition, several foot artillery companies were employed in garrison roles along the Atlantic coastline, stationed in local ports and fortifications. On 12 May 1814, the planned number of sixty foot artillery companies had not been reached, so the three regiments were consolidated into a single "Corps of Artillery" that comprised 12 battalions with four companies each (for a total of 48 companies). During the demobilization of 1815, the "Corps of Artillery" was reduced to 8 battalions with four companies each (for a total of 32 companies).

The US "Regiment of Light Artillery" was formed on 12 April 1808 and comprised ten companies, which were to perform as mounted artillery. During the war, however, not all the companies were always given horses due to the general lack of adequate mounts. When not mounted, the batteries of the "Regiment of Light Artillery" usually acted as normal field ones. Despite logistical problems, the unit performed quite well during the war against Britain and thus was retained after 1815. On paper the foot or horse batteries of the US artillery were to comprise six pieces: these could be four guns of the same calibre and two howitzers or six guns of not more than two different calibres.

THE US FOOT ARTILLERY, 1812

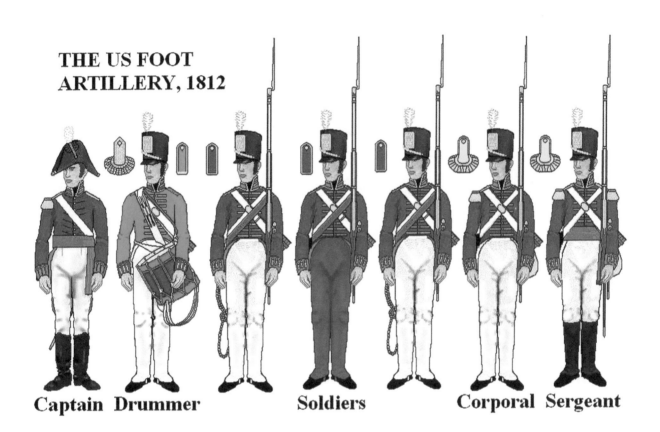

Captain Drummer Soldiers Corporal Sergeant

THE US FOOT ARTILLERY, 1813

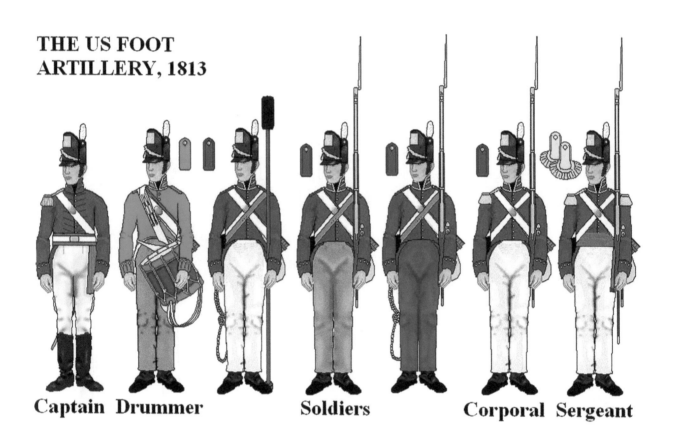

Captain Drummer   Soldiers   Corporal Sergeant

US LIGHT ARTILLERY
1812 - 1815

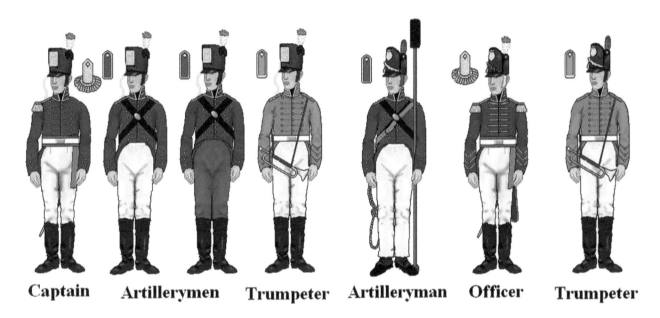

Captain   Artillerymen   Trumpeter   Artilleryman   Officer   Trumpeter

Uniforms adopted since 1814

The Engineer Corps

Since its foundation, on 16 March 1802, the Engineer Corps consisted of just a few specialist officers who had many different and difficult tasks to perform. This unit, in fact, was responsible for the construction and maintenance of all the fortifications and projects on the national territory of the US; in addition, the engineer officers were also responsible for the administration of West Point Academy (acting as instructors for the young cadets). In time of war the Engineer Corps was to be attached to the General Staff, in order to supervise the construction of all the structures needed by the military. During the war against Britain the engineer officers played a prominent part in the construction of new forts and in besieging operations. In April 1812, in order to face the needs of the upcoming conflict, the original establishment of the Engineer Corps was increased to 62 officers; in addition, during that same month, two "auxiliary" companies of enlisted men were created to support the engineer officers. The first of these, known as "Artificer Corps", was specialized in building of military structures and repairing of military materials; the second, instead, was called "Company of Bombardiers, Sappers and Miners". The "Artificer Corps" was recruited for a period of service of three years and thus was disbanded when the latter expired. The "Company of Bombardiers, Sappers and Miners", instead, was formally disbanded in 1823.

US CORPS OF ARTIFICERS
1812-1815

SUPERINTENDENT ADJUTANT OF THE SUPERINTENDENT MASTER WORKMEN WORKMAN

COY of SAPPERS, MINERS and BOMBARDIERS
1814-1815

OFFICER OF THE ENGINEER CORPS SAPPER DRUMMER

The Rangers

The American Rangers had a very long history, which dated back to 1676: in that year, during King Philip's War, Benjamin Church formed the first company of "rangers" to fight against the native tribes with their same hit-and-run tactics. During the following decades of the Colonial Period, the British Crown employed several ranger units in the military operations fought on the North American territory (most notably during the French-Indian War, which saw the colonial rangers playing a decisive role). In 1812, after a long period of absence, the Rangers were reformed as part of the independent American Army. They were created for use on the western frontier though they were not employed in conventional warfare against the British. Congress believed that most of the regular army would have been transferred on the border with Canada to fight the British and thus decided to form a special corps that could patrol in an effective way along the western frontier. Initially just six companies of frontiersmen were raised, for one year of service. These "special" soldiers were to act both on horse and on foot, due to the peculiar missions they had to carry out. All the rangers were marksmen and had a great knowledge of the terrain on which they fought. Their first responsibility was patrolling the frontier, in order to detect if the indigenous tribes could launch attacks against the settlers while most of the regular army was away fighting the British. In order to control the activities of the native tribes, the Rangers had to operate as "mounted infantrymen": this meant that they usually travelled long distances on horse but dismounted to fight in the woods. Five of the ranger companies were formed with volunteers coming from Ohio, Indiana, Illinois and Kentucky; the remaining one was recruited from frontiersmen of Tennessee. Each company comprised the following men: one captain, one lieutenant, one ensign, four sergeants, four corporals and 60 soldiers. Each man was responsible for his horse, weapons and personal equipment. Military discipline was not extremely rigid in the companies of Rangers, since these special frontier soldiers had to endure a very harsh daily life: they wore no uniforms and frequently fought with "guerrilla" methods, but from a formal point of view they were part of the regular army (albeit as temporary units, formed only for the duration of the war against Britain). The various companies never fought together, since they were dispersed across a vast territory. In January 1812 the terms of enlistment for the original six companies expired, but Congress decided to raise another ten companies of Rangers. These continued to serve for the rest of the war and were later increased to twelve by December 1813. At the end of the conflict, in June 1815, all the Ranger companies were discharged.

THE US RANGERS

Trumpeter **Rangers** **Officer** **Ranger**

The Marines and Sea Fencibles

During the War of 1812, the US Marines retained their previous organization with just one battalion; the latter's establishment, however, was slightly enlarged as the conflict progressed. The naval infantrymen had a primary mission of providing American warships with contingents of fusiliers, but the military emergencies happening during the war against Britain sometimes obliged them to fight on land as normal line infantrymen. In any case, because of their responsibilities on-board ships, the Marines always showed themselves to be an elite corps having excellent training and discipline.

It is interesting to note that the Marines were not the only unit from the US Navy to serve on land during the War of 1812. On 26 July 1813, Congress authorized the formation of a peculiar naval militia known as "Sea Fencibles". The latter comprised ten companies in total, which were to garrison the port installations and coastal fortifications that were located on the Atlantic. The men who made up the companies of Sea Fencibles were all volunteers, mostly civilian sailors who were temporarily unemployed due to the British naval blockade. Since most of the regular army's units were fighting on the frontiers, the Sea Fencibles were the main defenders of the American coasts. The ten companies, each of which numbered more or less 100 men, were distributed as follows: two in New York, two in Baltimore, two in Norfolk, two in Philadelphia and two in Boston. From a formal point of view, they formed a single battalion. Each company comprised the following men: one captain, one first lieutenant, one second lieutenant, one third lieutenant, one aspirant, twelve gunners and ninety rankers. The gunners of each company were specifically trained to operate as naval artillerymen. Quite strangely the officers of the Sea Fencibles came from the US Army, while their men were from the US Navy.

THE US MARINES

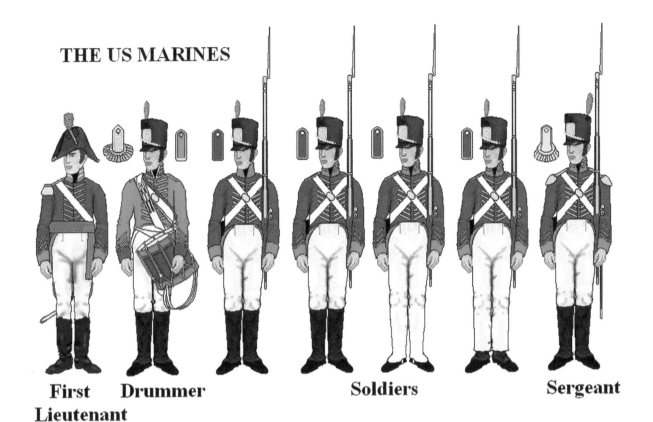

First Lieutenant **Drummer** **Soldiers** **Sergeant**

US NAVY AND SEA FENCIBLES

Captain **Lieutenants** **Aspirant** **Adjutant** **Sailors**

Chapter 3: The US Militia and Volunteers From 1812 to 1815

Historically the militias had always been a fundamental part of the US military and before that since the establishment of the early colonies during the first half of the 17th century. The British sent very few troops to garrison their colonies in North America and thus the early settlers of the future Thirteen Colonies soon had to organize themselves for defence of their lives and properties. This general situation led to the birth of the militia system in the US, which was quite simple but worked extremely well in the early years. Each able-bodied adult male could volunteer as a militiaman, who could be mobilized in case of need. In some cases, equipment was provided by the state and in others it was provided by the individual. This is usually the distinction between "state" troops and "local" militia. Both were raised from state cadres in time of war, but local militia usually only served in their home area, whereas state militia could be sent out of state. Both were organized for peacetime drills, but "state" troops had more formal training. Local militia had the reputation of being assembled in a few minutes and because of this the militiamen of the Revolution soon became known as "minutemen". Often the militia was made up of well-educated young men who wished to serve their local community in order to improve their social position. Under many points of view, the militia was a true "parallel army" that usually comprised much more men than the regular military forces. During the years of his presidency, George Washington had proposed to transform the state militias into a reserve military force that could be called to serve in case of military emergency: Congress, however, denied this proposal in order to defend the autonomy of the various federal territories. Many American political leaders, in fact, saw the militiamen as the only "real" defenders of the constitutional liberties (which could be menaced by the regular army). Generally speaking, the states of New England had the best militias in terms of quality and organization: in fact, these had been generally formed during the 17th century and thus had a long tradition of service. Militia companies were not controlled by the central government of Washington, but by their local authorities unless they were called into federal service, at which point they might be amalgamated with other local militia to form a state regiment - sometimes with each company in different uniforms. Infantry were the predominant branch of service because they were easy to form while more affluent communities might form cavalry and artillery units. The state militia was a very democratic military institution, since its members often choose their own officers (except for the superior ones). In some ways the position of militia officer was like the cursus honorum of ancient Rome – the path to political prominence. An outcome of this is that some higher officers had no experience or aptitude to commanding men once shooting started. States had an established organization, which might have been activated during the war, but then only some of these units might have been available for federal service.

Connecticut

The State of Connecticut had a well-organized militia, which included a good number of "active" units. They were assembled into four large "divisions", which numbered 12,582 men in total. Each division comprised two brigades having five infantry regiments of ten companies each. Differentiating them from the regular army, the companies that made up an infantry regiment had different tactical roles: eight were "centre" ones of fusiliers, while the remaining two were "flank" ones (one of grenadiers and one of chasseurs). In addition to the infantry regiments, the active militia comprised also several independent troops of cavalry and companies of artillery. During the war, 3,000 Connecticut active militiamen were called to serve in a special contingent known as "Military Corps for the Defence of the State". This force, which was ready to intervene in case of need, comprised the following units: two regiments of infantry, four troops of cavalry and four companies of artillery. It corresponded to a division, since it was composed by two brigades (each having one regiment of infantry, two troops of cavalry and two companies of artillery). In 1814 the establishment of the "Military Corps for the Defence of the State" was enlarged with the inclusion of four horse artillery companies (two for each brigade). In addition to the above, Connecticut could deploy also a certain number of volunteer units. The most famous of these was the "Governor's Guard", which was organized as two companies of infantry and two horse companies. Other volunteer units included the "Waterbury Volunteer Exempts" (a unit that was formed with men who were exempt from militia service), the "Milford Grenadiers" and the "Humphreyville Hussars".

CONNECTICUT MILITIA

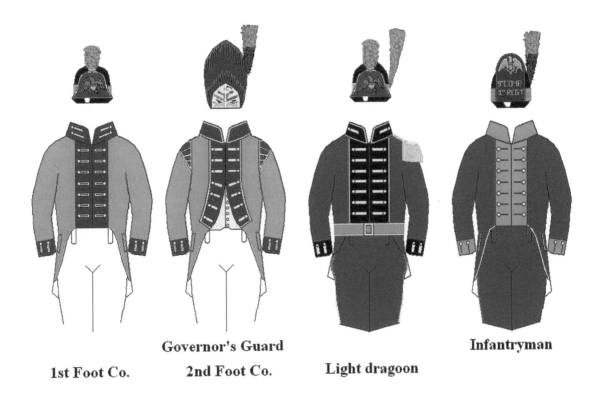

1st Foot Co.

Governor's Guard
2nd Foot Co.

Light dragoon

Infantryman

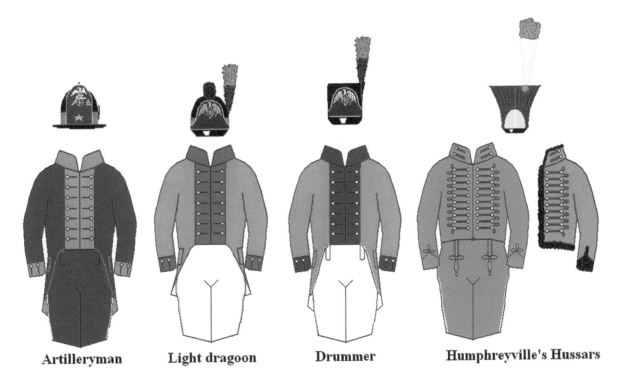

Artilleryman

Light dragoon

Drummer

Humphreyville's Hussars

Delaware

The state militia of Delaware consisted of a single division, which was structured on three brigades (one for each of Delaware's three counties). Each of the three brigades had a different internal composition, which included from a minimum of two to a maximum of eight infantry regiments plus at least one troop of cavalry and one company of artillery. The infantry regiments were made up of proper militiamen, while the cavalry troops and artillery companies were made up of volunteers. The infantry regiments were organized on two battalions, each having four companies of fusiliers and one "flank" company of grenadiers or chasseurs (which was to be formed by volunteers and not by ordinary militiamen). As clear from the above, most of the volunteers served in units that were part of the militia's organization; in any case, there is notice of a few "independent" volunteer corps. Two of these were formed in the city of Wilmington, the most important port of Delaware: an infantry company known as "Wilmington Light Infantry Blues" and an artillery company called "Wilmington Artillerists". Near Wilmington there was the important chemical industry of the Du Pont family, which produced most of the black powder employed by the US Army: since this productive site was of great strategic importance, it was defended by a specific volunteer corps known as "Brandywine Rangers" (organized by the Du Pont family).

DELAWARE MILITIA

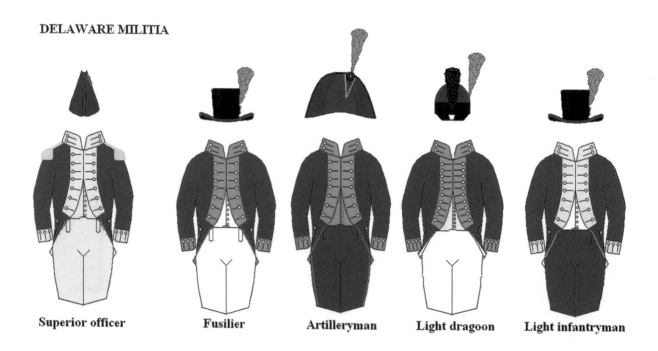

| Superior officer | Fusilier | Artilleryman | Light dragoon | Light infantryman |

District of Columbia

The District of Columbia was created in 1800 and comprised the federal capital city of Washington, which was separated from all the bordering states. Despite having a very little territory and population, the District of Columbia had its own militia that comprised two "legions": the "1st Militia Legion of Washington" and the "2nd Militia Legion of Alexandria"; the first of these comprised two regiments of infantry and one squadron of cavalry, while the second had one regiment of infantry and one regiment of cavalry (light dragoons). On 17 April 1813 the two "legions" were transformed into brigades and assembled together in order to form a single division. In addition to the above, there were also some independent companies of volunteers (these being of light infantry, rifles or artillery).

DISTRICT OF COLUMBIA MILITIA

Colonel of infantry   Infantryman   Alexandria Light Dragoons   Artilleryman   Washington Light Dragoons

Georgia

Georgia had the southern border in common with Spanish Florida and thus was one of the states that were always under a potential threat of foreign attack. In addition, in the western part of the state, there were frequent tensions with the powerful Creeks. As a result of the above, the state militia of Georgia was well organized and a large number of trained men. From 1807 each of the counties that made up the state had to provide one or two infantry regiments according to its population; as a result, there were a total of 32 infantry regiments. These were assembled into four divisions, which comprised two brigades each; a single brigade had four regiments of infantry. In December 1812 another infantry division was created, having the same establishment of the existing ones. The cavalry was organized in an independent brigade since 1808: this comprised 13 "regiments", each formed by just two troops. Each of the 26 counties had to provide one cavalry troop. The military formations of Georgia included several units of volunteers, mostly formed in the city of Savannah: "Savannah Volunteer Guards", "Republican Blues", "Independent Blues", "Liberty Independent Troop", "Chatam Rangers", "Chatam Light Dragoons", "Chatam Hussars", "Conner's Mounted Riflemen", "Chatam Artillery" and "Savannah Heavy Artillery".

GEORGIA MILITIA

| General officer | Infantryman | Light Dragoons of Chatham | Artilleryman | Mounted Rifleman |

Indiana

The Indiana Territory was created in 1800 and only became a state in 1816, after the end of the war with Britain. Despite this, the militiamen from this region played an important role during the military operations against Tecumseh and his native warriors. Until 1811 the infantry regiments of the Indiana state militia had been distinguished according to their county of origin. In that year, however, the various units started to be numbered in progressive order and lost their previous designation. On 3 January 1814 there was a further reorganization, which prescribed that an average infantry company was to comprise 60 men; however, a single company could have from a minimum of 40 rankers to a maximum of 80. A battalion was made up of a minimum of two to a maximum of seven companies; two battalions made up a regiment. One company of each regiment was to consist of the best and youngest militiamen, who were defined as grenadiers or chasseurs (thus forming an elite "flank" company). The regiments were assembled into brigades: the latter could have from a minimum of two to a maximum of eight regiments. Brigades could be assembled into divisions, which could contain from a minimum of two to a maximum of four brigades. The adoption of the new organization resulted in the formation of three infantry divisions, each with two brigades of two regiments (for a total of 12 infantry regiments). One company of rifles, one troop of cavalry and one battery of artillery were attached to each infantry brigade (being formed with volunteers).

INDIANA MILITIA

General officer   **Mounted Ranger**   **Militiaman**   **Officer**   **Light Dragoon**   **Militiaman**

Kentucky

Kentucky was one of the youngest American states, having been established in 1792: as a result, by the outbreak of the war with Britain, the inhabitants of this frontier region still lived as backwater settlers and were used to harsh living conditions. Despite being few proportionally in number and generally poor, the Kentuckians contributed several thousand militiamen to the American war effort. According to the organization established in 1792, the militia of Kentucky was organized into two divisions: the first comprised the militiamen coming from that part of the state that was located south of the Kentucky River; the second comprised of militiamen coming from that part of the state that was located north of the Kentucky River. Each of the two divisions comprised two brigades; the brigades were made up of the following infantry regiments: 1st Brigade had five regiments (numbered 1 to 5) coming from the counties of Jefferson, Shelby, Nelson, Washington and Logan; 2nd Brigade had two regiments (numbered 6 to 7) coming from the counties of Lincoln, Madison and Mercer; 3rd Brigade had four regiments (numbered 8 to 11) coming from the counties of Fayette and Woodford; 4th Brigade had four regiments (numbered 12 to 15) coming from the counties of Scott, Bourbon and Mason. Each nfantry regiment was divided into two battalions and each battalion had five companies. In addition to the above, the militia of Kentucky comprised also several independent units of volunteers: these were regiments of rifles and companies of cavalry or artillery. The most famous volunteer corps formed in Kentucky was the "Regiment of Kentucky Mounted Volunteers", created by the valorous Colonel Johnson on 22 March 1813. This unit consisted of "mounted riflemen", who were equipped as the regular Rangers and acted as an elite corps of mounted infantry. On 5 October 1813, at the Battle of the River Raisin, these volunteers were able to break the line of the British 41st Regiment of Foot and their commander (Johnson) killed the great native leader Tecumseh. The regiment comprised a total of eight companies.

KENTUCKY MILITIA

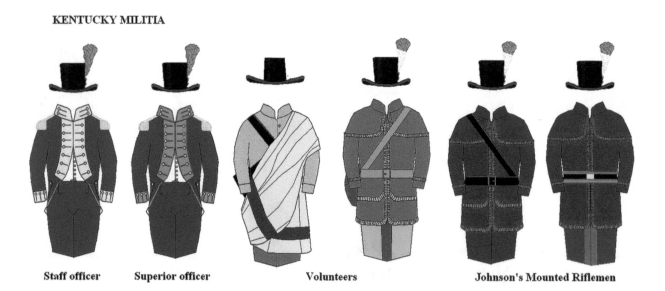

Staff officer   Superior officer   Volunteers   Johnson's Mounted Riflemen

Louisiana

Louisiana became a state on 30 April 1812, after being divided into several independent "territories" since 1803. At the time of the US annexation, the Louisiana militia was already well organized: both the Spanish and the French, in fact, had always dedicated great resources to the defence of such a large territory. The militia was well structured especially in New Orleans, since that important city was almost constantly menaced by naval squadrons of the European powers. Until 24 February 1813, the New Orleans militia comprised two regiments of infantry and a small police corps of "gendarmes"; on that date, the whole Louisiana militia was reorganized on two divisions with ten infantry regiments each. The 1st Division included regiments raised from the southern part of Louisiana and New Orleans, while the 2nd Division included regiments raised from the central and northern parts of the state. Cavalry was structured on just five troops. In addition to the above, various volunteer corps existed in New Orleans (which inhabitants were mostly French); the most important of these were the "Battalion of Orleans Volunteers" (infantry) and the "Orleans Troop of Horse" (cavalry). By late 1814 most of the minor volunteer units existing in New Orleans were absorbed into the "Battalion of Orleans Volunteers" (which by now comprised five companies and a detachment of sappers). Each of the five companies was formed by volunteers having the same ethnic origin: the "Grenadiers Company", "Foot Dragoons Company", "Francs Company" and "Chasseurs Company" were all made up of Frenchmen, while the "Louisiana Blues Company" (previously an independent unit) was made up of Irish-Americans. In addition to the "Battalion of Orleans Volunteers", there were also other two "ethnic" units formed with free blacks who wished to serve as volunteers: these were respectively known as "Louisiana Coloured Battalion" and "Saint-Domingue Coloured Battalion". The first had a total of four companies (two of fusiliers, one of grenadiers and one of chasseurs) while the second had five ones (three of fusiliers, one of grenadiers and one of chasseurs). Smaller independent units of volunteers comprised the "Orleans Rifle Company", which was made up of American marksmen. The artillery of New Orleans' militia was entirely provided by volunteers, who were organized in two different units: a company of "Cannoniers-Bombardiers" (comprising men of French origin) and a company of "Washington Artillery" (comprising men of American origin). In addition to these, there were the irregular corsairs provided by the famous pirate Jean Lafitte (who supported the American government with his men during the British attack against New Orleans). These were all excellent gunners, who had a lot of experience in the field of naval warfare.

LOUISIANA MILITIA

General
officer

Officer
Grenadier Company

Grenadier
Orleans Volunteers

Rifleman
Louisiana Blues

Orleans
Rifle
Company

Cannoniers-
Bombardiers

Maryland

The militia of Maryland was very well organized and had a long military tradition dating back to the 17th century. By the outbreak of the war with Britain, it was structured on three infantry divisions: the 1st had two regiments of infantry, two companies of riflemen, two troops of cavalry and two companies of artillery; the 2nd had three regiments of infantry, two companies of riflemen, three troops of cavalry and two companies of artillery; the 3rd had three regiments of infantry, three companies of riflemen, three troops of cavalry and one company of artillery. Infantry regiments were formed according to counties, while the cavalry troops were raised according to the following system: Maryland was divided into 11 cavalry districts and a certain number of these were assigned to each of the three infantry divisions, having to provide two or three troops of horse to it. In 1814 the infantry establishment of each unit was expanded, and the regiments were organized in brigades. The brigades were formed by assembling a certain number of regiments, coming from several counties of the state; each county deployed a different number of infantry regiments according to its population: 1st Division (made up of 2nd, 4th, 5th, 7th, 8th and 9th Brigades); 2nd Division (made up of 1st, 6th, 10th and 12th Brigades); 3rd Division (made up of

3rd, 11th and 13th Brigades). The internal organization of the brigades was as follows: 1st Brigade had four regiments from the counties of Cecil and Harford; 2nd Brigade had four regiments from the counties of Allegany and Washington; 3rd Brigade had five regiments and an independent rifle battalion with three companies from Baltimore City; 4th Brigade had four regiments from the counties of Prince George and Lower Montgomery; 5th Brigade had four regiments from the counties of Saint Mary and Charles; 6th Brigade had four regiments from the counties of Kent and Queen Anne; 7th Brigade had four regiments from the counties of Upper Montgomery and Lower Frederick; 8th Brigade had four regiments from the counties of Calvert and Anne Arundel; 9th Brigade had four regiments from the county of Upper Frederick; 10th Brigade had four regiments from the counties of Lower Worcester, Upper Worcester and Somerset; 11th Brigade had four regiments from Baltimore County; the 12th Brigade had four regiments from the counties of Caroline, Dorchester and Talbot; the 13th Brigade had two regiments from the county of Bladensburg. In total, 51 regiments and 1 rifle battalion. The city of Baltimore had several units of volunteers: "Baltimore Independent Blues", "Hibernian Corps of Union Greens", "Hibernian Infantry", "First Baltimore Light Infantry", "Second Baltimore Light Infantry", "First Baltimore Rifle Company", "Second Baltimore Rifle Company" and "Baltimore Hussars".

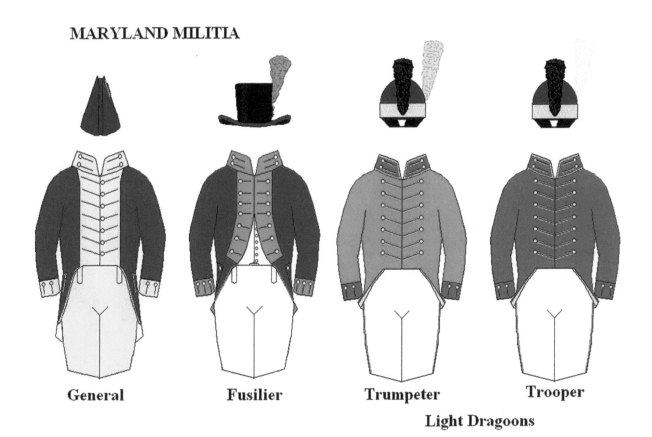

MARYLAND MILITIA

General   **Fusilier**   **Trumpeter**   **Trooper**

Light Dragoons

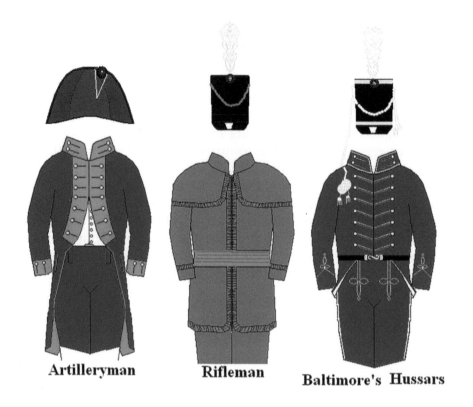

Artilleryman   **Rifleman**   **Baltimore's Hussars**

MARYLAND MILITIA

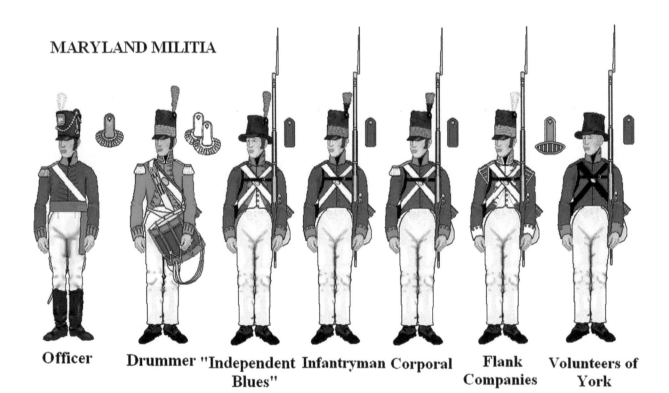

Officer   **Drummer "Independent Blues"**   **Infantryman**   **Corporal**   **Flank Companies**   **Volunteers of York**

Massachusetts

Before analysing the structure of Massachusetts' militia, it is important to remember that until 1820 this state also comprised the territory of Maine (which was simply known as "District of Maine"). The politicians of Massachusetts were contrary to the war against Britain, since they were sure that the latter would have severely damaged their economy (which benefitted a lot from international commerce). As a result of this situation, Massachusetts decided that its militia units could be employed only inside the borders of the state (in order to avoid involvement in offensive operations conducted against the British). This decision caused serious troubles to the central government, since Massachusetts probably had the best militia organization among those of the various American states and territories. The infantry was structured on 13 divisions (six raised in Maine), which were in turn organized on four brigades; each of the latter was to comprise four regiments and each regiment had ten companies. The single average company was to number 60 men. Infantry regiments were recruited on a county basis, while the cavalry was raised according to another system: each infantry brigade was to have two or three cavalry companies, which were assembled to form a single squadron. The cavalry companies were recruited from "cavalry districts", which were formed by assembling several counties of the state. Similarly, each infantry brigade was to have two attached companies of artillery. One or two companies of light infantry, formed by volunteers, were also attached to each infantry brigade. In addition to the above Boston, the most important city of Massachusetts, could also count on several units of volunteers who were generally well equipped: "Ancient and Honourable Artillery Company", "Company of Independent Boston Fusiliers", "New England Guards", "Boston Independent Cadets", "Boston Light Dragoons" and "Boston Hussars". Smaller areas of the state also organized units of volunteers: "Salem Independent Cadets", "Salem Light Infantry Company", "Company of Washington Rangers", "Salem Artillery Company", "Washington Blues", "Salem Mechanic Light Infantry", "Marblehead Light Infantry Company", "Independent Gloucester Artillery", "Roxbury Artillery" and "Northampton Artillery". The "District of Maine" had several volunteer corps: "Portland Light Infantry Company", "Portland Rifle Company", "Bath Light Infantry Company", "Wells Cavalry Troop", "Kennebunk Cavalry Troop", "Bath Artillery Company" and "Saco Artillery Company".

MASSACHUSETTS MILITIA

General
officer

Infantryman

Boston
Independent
Cadets

Honourable
Artillery
Company

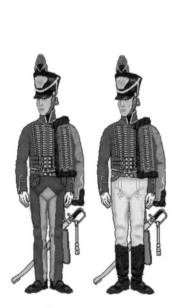  

Boston Hussars

Light
infantryman

Boston
Independent
Fusiliers

Michigan

In 1812 Michigan was still a territory and not a state; despite this, it had a small but well-organized militia (which was created in 1805). The latter comprised the following units: "1st Regiment of Infantry" (with 8 companies, from Detroit and the surrounding areas), "2nd Regiment of Infantry" (with 7 companies of infantry and 1 of cavalry, from the Erie District), one battalion of infantry (with 4 companies) from the Huron District and two companies of infantry from Michilimackinak. In addition to the above, there was a volunteer "Legionary Corps" that was raised from the area of Detroit; this comprised one company of light infantry, one company of rifles, one company of cavalry and one company of artillery.

MICHIGAN MILITIA

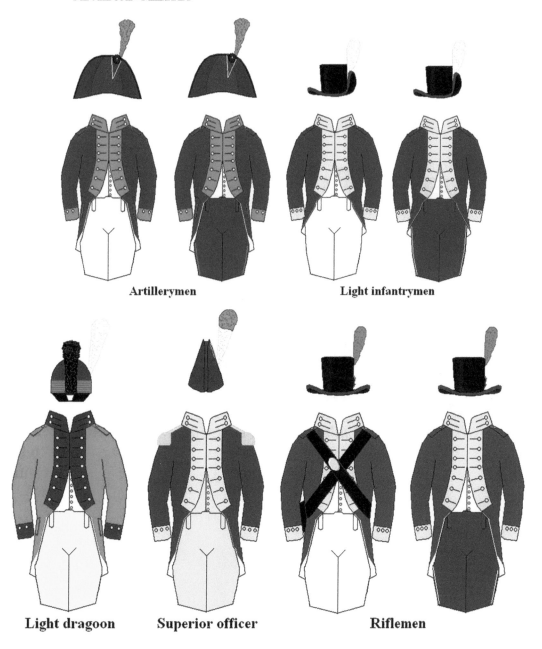

Artillerymen   Light infantrymen

Light dragoon   Superior officer   Riflemen

Mississippi

The Territory of Mississippi was created in 1798 and became a state only in 1817. Each of its counties was to have an infantry regiment with two battalions and at least one troop of cavalry: as a result, there were a total of 18 infantry regiments. In addition to the above, there were also several volunteer units that were attached to the militia: these could be independent companies of light infantry or rifles; a single volunteer artillery company existed at Natchez (where also a company of rifles was raised). During the war, from September to December 1813, four of the existing cavalry troops (each with more or less 50 men) were assembled to form a squadron of "Mississippi Dragoons". This unit was embodied again in 1814 and took part to the defence of New Orleans during the following year.

MISSISSIPPI MILITIA

General officer   Infantryman   Light Dragoon   Light Dragoon of Adams County   Militiaman   Light Dragoon of Jefferson County

New Jersey

According to the Militia Act of 1792, each county of New Jersey was to form a certain number of militia companies: these could be of fusiliers, grenadiers, light infantry, cavalry or artillery and were assembled into larger units only in case of "activation". Compared with those of other American states, the military forces of New Jersey were not particularly numerous; only 3,500 militiamen from this state were "activated" during the War of 1812 against Britain. According to the Militia Act of 1792, a regiment of infantry was to comprise a total of ten companies: only one or two of these could be "flank" ones (with grenadiers or light infantrymen). Five companies made up a battalion, since each regiment was structured on two battalions. Four troops of cavalry could be assembled to form a squadron; sometimes squadrons could be consolidated into regiments. Regarding the artillery, there was a limit of eight companies for the whole state; these were assembled into a single regiment having two battalions of four companies. The first independent companies of riflemen started to be created since February 1812. In addition to the above, there were also some volunteer corps: "Chatham Fusiliers", "Morris Rangers" and "Bottle Hill Riflemen".

NEW JERSEY MILITIA

| General | Quartermaster | Light dragoon | Fusilier | Grenadier |

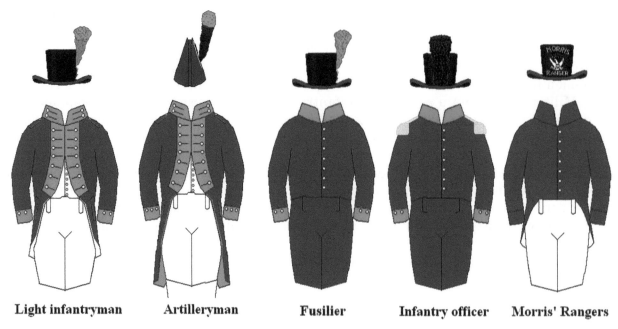

Light infantryman   **Artilleryman**   **Fusilier**   **Infantry officer**   **Morris' Rangers**

New uniforms

New Hampshire

The Militia Act of 1808 reorganized the militia of New Hampshire on three divisions, each of the latter comprising two brigades. Each brigade had a certain number of infantry regiments; these were formed on a county basis according to the population of each administrative district. In total, there were 37 infantry regiments; these were organized on standard battalions, which included flank companies of grenadiers and light infantrymen that were made up of volunteers. A troop of cavalry and a company of artillery, formed by volunteers, were attached to several of the infantry regiments. The troops of cavalry could be assembled to form three regiments of "light horse". Since 16 June 1810 the militia of New Hampshire comprised also a "Company of Horse Artillery", which was unique among the various militia units of the American states.

New York

New York had a long border in common with British Canada and thus was heavily involved into the military campaigns of 1812-1815. Even before the outbreak of the war, New York had a strong militia organization; being well drilled and equipped, was greatly expanded during the conflict. In total, the New York militia of 1812 comprised the following units: 159 infantry regiments assembled into 40 brigades, 9 cavalry regiments assembled into 3 brigades and several regiments or companies of artillery. Only a small part of these militia corps, however, was made up of "active" units that were called to serve; the active units were organized into two large divisions as follows: "1st Division" with 1st, 2nd, 3rd and 4th Brigades; "2nd Division" with 5th, 6th, 7th and 8th Brigades. The brigades comprised the following "active" regiments: the "1st Brigade" had 1st New York City Regiment, 2nd New York City Regiment and 3rd Queens Regiment; "2nd Brigade" had 4th Ulster Regiment, 5th Dutchess Regiment and 6th Dutchess Regiment; "3rd Brigade" had 7th Washington Regiment, 8th Clinton Regiment and 9th Columbia Regiment; "4th Brigade" had 10th Saratoga Regiment, 11th Schoharie Regiment, 12th Albany Regiment and 13th Delaware Regiment; "5th Brigade" had 14th Oneida Regiment and 15th Saint Lawrence Regiment; "6th Brigade" had 16th Ostego Regiment and 17th Chenango Regiment; "7th Brigade" had 18th Seneca Regiment, 19th Cayuga Regiment and 20th Ontario Regiment; "8th Brigade" was made up of light infantry and riflemen units. The artillery of New York comprised a total of 13 militia regiments (formed with companies coming from the various counties) and an independent volunteer company known as "Veteran Corps of Artillery". In addition, from 9 May 1814, the militia of New York also comprised an elite corps known as "Governor's Guard Battalion" (which acted as personal escort for the Governor of New York State). In 1817, after the end of the war, this corps became the new 14th regiment of the militia artillery. Obviously, the state of New York deployed many units of volunteers: "Troy Fusiliers", "Troy Invincibles", "Republican Greens" (a battalion of Irishmen), "Albany Republican Greens", "Republican Blues", "Brooklyn Fusiliers", "Iron Greys", "Ontario County Rifle Company", "Trojan Greens Rifle Company", "Unadilla Rifle Company", "Rochester Dragoons" and "Orange Hussars". Later in the war, some independent volunteer corps of rifles were assembled in order to form the new "1st Regiment of New York Riflemen".

NEW YORK MILITIA

Senior
officer

Infantryman

7th

8th

Light Dragoons

Artilleryman Drummer

Governor's Guard

Trojan
Rifles

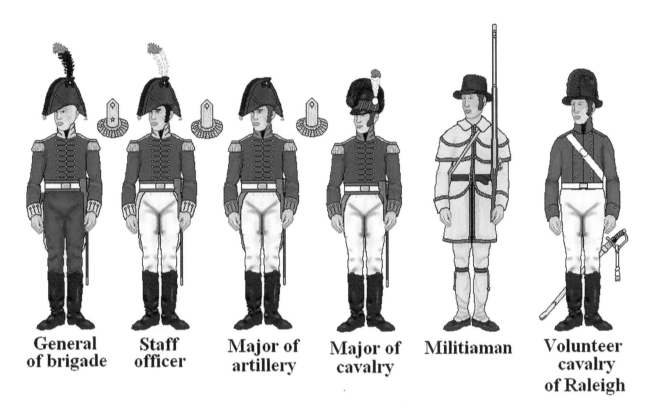

| General of brigade | Staff officer | Major of artillery | Major of cavalry | Militiaman | Volunteer cavalry of Raleigh |

North Carolina

When war with Britain broke out in 1812, North Carolina was requested to activate a total of 7,000 militiamen: these were organized into just two brigades, each composed of four infantry regiments. In addition, the following units were also formed for active service: one regiment of riflemen, one regiment of cavalry and one regiment of artillery. The 1st Brigade comprised the following units: 1st Regiment of North Carolina Militia (with 10 companies), 2nd Regiment of North Carolina Militia (with 12 companies), 3rd Regiment of North Carolina Militia (with 8 companies) and 4th Regiment of North Carolina Militia (with 11 companies). The 2nd Brigade comprised the following units: 5th Regiment of North Carolina Militia (with 11 companies), 6th Regiment of North Carolina Militia (with 6 companies), 7th Regiment of North Carolina Militia (with 10 companies) and 8th Regiment of North Carolina Militia (with companies). The "Regiment of Riflemen" was structured on 6 companies, while the "Regiment of Cavalry" had 9 ones. The "Regiment of Artillery", instead, consisted of just 5 companies. In 1814 the militia of North Carolina was completely reorganized and the following units were "activated": 1st Regiment of North Carolina Militia (with 13 companies), 2nd Regiment of North Carolina Militia (with 14 companies), 3rd Regiment of North Carolina Militia (with 14 companies), 4th Regiment of North Carolina Militia (with 11 companies), 5th Regiment of North Carolina Militia (with 12 companies), 6th Regiment of North Carolina Militia (with 10 companies) and 7th Regiment of North Carolina Militia (with 12 companies).

OHIO MILITIA

Senior officer   **Junior officer**   **Militiaman**   **Infantryman**

Ohio

Ohio was a very young state, having been created in 1803. In 1812 the Ohio region was still a frontier area, where the natives represented the main military menace. The militia of this new state started to be organized from 1809: in that year, in fact, it was established that all the able-bodied men had to serve as militiamen in independent infantry companies. During the spring of 1812, due to the outbreak of the war with Britain, the state authorities of Ohio decided to "activate" a good number of the infantry companies and assembled them into three new "Regiments of Ohio Volunteers". Similarly, to what happened in Kentucky and Mississippi, the men from Ohio's militia were mostly frontiersmen many equipped with rifled muskets.

Pennsylvania

According to the new organization established on 12 May 1812, the militia of Pennsylvania comprise a total of 14,000 men assembled into two divisions. Each of these comprised two brigades formed by a varying number of infantry regiments; in total, there were 22 regiments. One of the four brigades, numbering more or less 3,000 militiamen, was known as "Advanced Light Brigade". Regiments of infantry were composed of "flank" companies of light infantrymen. Two companies of rifles, one troop of cavalry and one company of artillery (all formed by volunteers) were attached to each infantry brigade. As a result of the above, the 14,000 militiamen deployed by Pennsylvania were divided as follows: 11,200 infantrymen, 1,400 riflemen, 700 cavalrymen and 700 artillerymen. Obviously, in addition to the above, there were some volunteer units (most of which were created in the city of Philadelphia): "Mercer Blues", "State Guards", "First Troops of Philadelphia Cavalry" and "Montgomery County Troop of Cavalry".

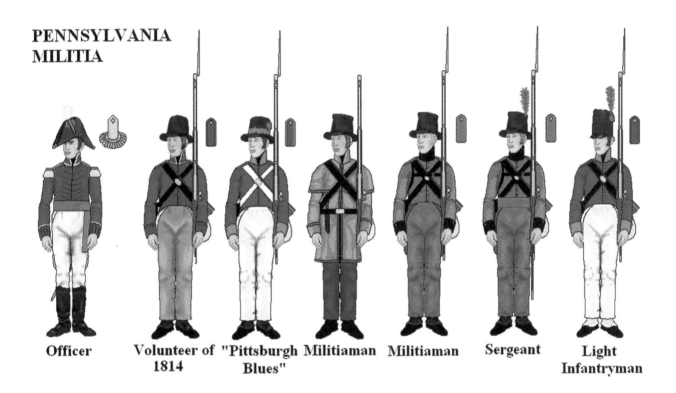

PENNSYLVANIA MILITIA

Officer — Volunteer of 1814 — "Pittsburgh Blues" — Militiaman — Militiaman — Sergeant — Light Infantryman

Rhode Island

Being a very small state, Rhode Island had a very peculiar militia system compared with those of the other American states. Formally, like in all the other states and territories, all the able-bodied men of Rhode Island had to serve in the general militia; in practice, however, the militia of Rhode Island was entirely formed by small companies of volunteers that received charters from the state government in order to organize themselves for local defence. As a result, every 5-10 years, some new company-sized units were chartered while those that had been chartered during the previous years were discharged. In 1812 the following five volunteer units made up the militia of Rhode Island: "Warwick and Coventry Guards", "Union Guards of Providence", "Washington Guards", "Cumberland and Smithfield Light Dragoons" and "Hazard's Artillery". With the progression of the war, however, the number of chartered corps was increased to 30 and a division with four infantry "brigades" was formed (with brigades being raised on a county basis). 1st Brigade was formed from Newport and Bristol County; 2nd Brigade was formed from Providence County; 3rd Brigade was formed from Washington County; 4th Brigade was formed from Kent County. Among the new chartered units there was also a "Special State Corps" comprising four companies. The company-sized units of volunteers included also corps of light infantry and artillery, as well as a single company of naval artillery that was stationed in Providence (the "Providence Marine Corps of Artillery").

RHODE ISLAND MILITIA

Providence Marine Corps of Artillery   Newport Guard   Newport Artillery   Kent Artillery   Providence light infantry

South Carolina

The militia of South Carolina was organized into two divisions, one comprising five infantry brigades and the other comprising just four. In total the two divisions deployed 39 regiments, since the various brigades had different internal structures. Infantry regiments generally had ten companies. The cavalry comprised 8 regiments and 1 squadron, while the artillery had 1 regiment and 1 battalion. In addition to the above, there were also some artillery companies attached to the brigades of infantry. On 30 December 1814 a brigade of the militia was "activated" in order to fight against the British - this was to comprise just two infantry regiments, each having two battalions with five companies. The city of Charleston had two independent units of volunteers: "Charleston Light Dragoons" and "Charleston Artillery".

SOUTH CAROLINA MILITIA

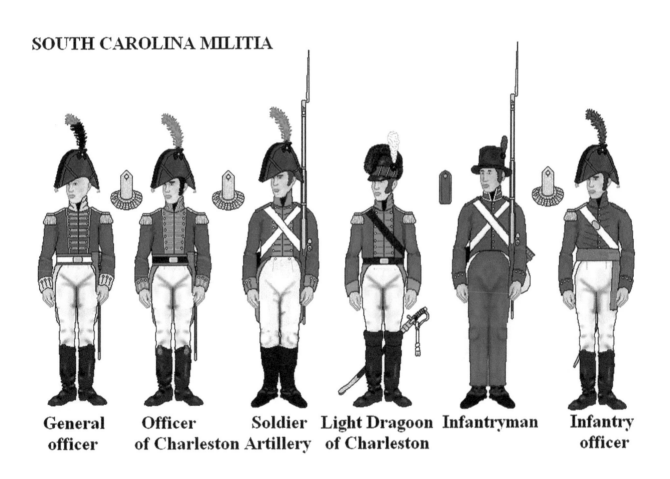

General officer   Officer of Charleston Artillery   Soldier of Charleston   Light Dragoon of Charleston   Infantryman   Infantry officer

Tennessee

The State of Tennessee was created in 1792 and thus was one of the youngest "frontier" states. Despite this, the contribution given by Tennessee to the US war effort was quite significant. During the conflict, militia infantry of this state changed organization several times but continued to be structured on several regiments plus some independent battalions. The regiments of infantry were divided among units coming from Western Tennessee and units coming from Eastern Tennessee; their geographical provenance was indicated in their official denomination. Each infantry regiment was to include a company of light infantrymen and a company of riflemen. Cavalry was entirely made up of "mounted riflemen" units, which were defined as "mounted infantry" or "mounted gunmen" due to their peculiar tactical function – essentially acting as true dragoons. The soldiers of these corps fought like the Rangers of the regular army and were all experienced marksmen. This category of troops was very popular in the militias of the frontier states like Kentucky or Tennessee. The artillery of Tennessee was limited from a numerical point of view, consisting of a single volunteer company.

TENNESSEE MILITIA

| General | Infantryman | Militiaman | Officer | Artilleryman |

Vermont

The militia of Vermont was organized into just one brigade, which comprised four regiments of infantry with eight companies each; one company of cavalry and one company of artillery were attached to each infantry regiment. In November 1812 the militia was reorganized and expanded, reaching an establishment of 64 infantry and 2 cavalry companies. In addition to the above there were also independent companies of light infantrymen and riflemen, which could be attached to the regiments of infantry. Finally, there were some volunteer artillery units: "Washington Artillery of Montpellier" (which acted as the governor's guard of Vermont), "Hartland Artillery Company" and "Barnard Artillery Company".

VERMONT MILITIA

| General officer | Artilleryman | Rifleman | Militiaman | Light Dragoon | Barnard Light Dragoons |

Virginia

In 1812 Virginia had a well-organized militia, which comprised many units that were fully equipped and uniformed. The militia of Virginia had a long tradition of activity stretching back to the early decades of the 17th century at the beginning of the Colonial Period. All able-bodied men of the state were to serve in the general militia, which was structured on county regiments (each county providing one or more infantry regiments according to its population). Each infantry regiment comprised "flank" companies of grenadiers and light infantrymen. All the existing regiments were organized into 21 infantry brigades, which were in turn organized into 4 large divisions. Each infantry brigade had some attached independent units, made up of volunteers: companies of rifles, troops of cavalry and companies of artillery. Some of the most important volunteer corps were the following: "Petersburg Volunteers", "Richmond Light Infantry Blues", "Johnson's Company of Riflemen" and "Norfolk Artillery". In addition, there was also an "Independent Corps of Artificers" that served in the state's manufactory of arms in Richmond. Finally, always in Richmond, there was also a small corps of "gendarmerie" known as "Public Guard" (with 68 officers and men). Both the "Independent Corps of Artificers" and the "Public Guard" were not part of the militia but were considered as "regular" military units of Virginia (something that was very peculiar, since no other state had a body of regular troops).

VIRGINIA MILITIA

| General officer | Light infantryman | Light Dragoon | Artilleryman | Rifleman | Militiaman | Infantryman 1813 |

Chapter 4: The British Army in Canada from 1812 to 1815

When the United States became independent in 1783, Britain was able to retain possession of Canada and of other minor colonies located in North America. They were administratively divided as follows: Lower Canada, Upper Canada, Nova Scotia, New Brunswick, Newfoundland, Prince Edward Island and Cape Breton Island. The economies of all these territories had a precise role in the global commercial system created by Britain centred around fur trade, fishing and wood exports. During the long wars against Revolutionary and Napoleonic France, Canada became extremely important for Britain as a source of high-quality wood for building warships. In general, the territory of Canada was not as economically developed as that of the USA, but its population (albeit being quite small) was made up of people loyal to the crown. The troops garrisoning Canada during 1812-1815 were of three different kinds: British regular units, Canadian militia and Canadian volunteer units. The British regulars of those years were probably the best soldiers in the world, but the Canadian militiamen and volunteers also proved to be excellent fighters. The British regulars included some "foreign" units (Swiss infantry regiments) and colonial ones coming from other overseas territories (the "West India Regiments"). The militia system of Canada derived from the French colonial period and remained extremely efficient under the British, as the US Army would soon learn during the war. In 1812, at the outbreak of the war with the US, the British regular military units stationed in Canada were numerically small consisting of just 6,034 men and included the following corps:

- 8th Regiment of Foot (1st Battalion in Canada, 2nd Battalion in Nova Scotia and New Brunswick)
- 41st Regiment of Foot
- 49th Regiment of Foot
- 100th Regiment of Foot
- Six companies of the 98th Regiment of Foot (in Nova Scotia)
- Four companies of the 99th Regiment of Foot (in Nova Scotia)
- 10th "Royal Veteran" Battalion
- Detachments of the Royal Artillery
- Detachments of the Royal Engineers
- Detachments of the Royal Military Artificers/Royal Sappers and Miners
- "Canadian Regiment of Fencibles"
- "Nova Scotia Regiment of Fencibles"
- "New Brunswick Regiment of Fencibles" (later 104th Regiment of Foot)
- "Royal Newfoundland Regiment of Fencibles"

The British regular garrison included no cavalry units and just small detachments of the "technical corps" (artillery, engineers, artificers/sappers and miners). The core of the British troops in North America was represented by the 41st and 49th Regiments of Foot, which had been garrisoned in Canada for some time. These two units had learned how to fight in the woods of North America and had a special relation with the local population.

Line infantry and Fencibles

The British regiments of line infantry consisted of one or two battalions (though some had multiple battalions that acted independently), each with ten companies (8 of fusiliers, 1 of grenadiers and 1 of light infantry). In addition to these there were independent "veteran" battalions, like the 10th "Royal Veteran" Battalion that was a peculiar unit being formed with invalids who were no longer fit for front line military service; during the Napoleonic Wars, due to the high number of invalids who remained available for military service, various European armies of the time developed units of this kind. The "veteran" battalions of the British Army started to be formed around 1802, initially having the derogatory name of "Invalid" battalions. By the end of 1806 there were nine "veteran" battalions in the British Army; in December of that year a 10th Battalion was formed specifically for service in Canada, with volunteers coming from the nine existing units. These experienced soldiers went to serve in North America with the promise of receiving some land in Canada upon their retirement or at the disbandment of their unit. The units of "Fencibles", despite being part of the British regular forces, had a distinctive character that made them similar to the militia. The term "Fencibles" derived from the word "defencible", since these were units formed specifically for the defence of a certain territory. They were "fixed" garrison corps, having static nature: since these troops were recruited on a local basis, they had strong links with their home territory albeit being part of the British regular military forces.

The "Canadian Regiment of Fencibles" was formed in 1803, being initially made up of Scottish volunteers who had revolted against the Crown prior to being sent to Canada; it numbered around 600 men, who made up a total of ten companies (8 of fusiliers, 1 of grenadiers and 1 of light infantry). In practice, the unit had the normal establishment of a battalion despite having the denomination of "regiment". The "Nova Scotia Regiment of Fencibles" was raised on 9 July 1803 and had the same internal structure of the "Canadian Regiment of Fencibles". The "New Brunswick Regiment of Fencibles" was formed in August 1803 and had the same organization of a normal line infantry battalion; differently from those of the other units, the members of this corps accepted to serve also outside their home territory and thus the regiment was later transformed into a unit of the British line infantry (the 104th Regiment of Foot, in 1810). In contrast to the other regiments of "Fencibles" that were stationed in North America, which were all disbanded in 1816, this unit existed until 1817. To replace the 104th Regiment of Foot, a new "New Brunswick Regiment of Fencibles" was raised in October 1812 (having same establishment of the previous unit but being equipped with light infantry muskets). The "Royal Newfoundland Regiment of Fencibles" was created on 6 June 1812: formally it had to be a "proper" regiment, but always had the establishment of a single battalion. In addition to the "Fencibles", the British formed also another peculiar unit having as main objective that of garrisoning key locations in Canada. Created in September 1812, this was known as "Independent Companies of Foreigners". It was also called "French Independent Companies", since they were made up of French deserters and prisoners of war (who were transferred from England to Canada). The corps comprised just two companies, which soon became famous for their scarce discipline; its men had uniforms and weapons of the light infantry. The "Independent Companies of Foreigners" were eventually disbanded in early May 1814.

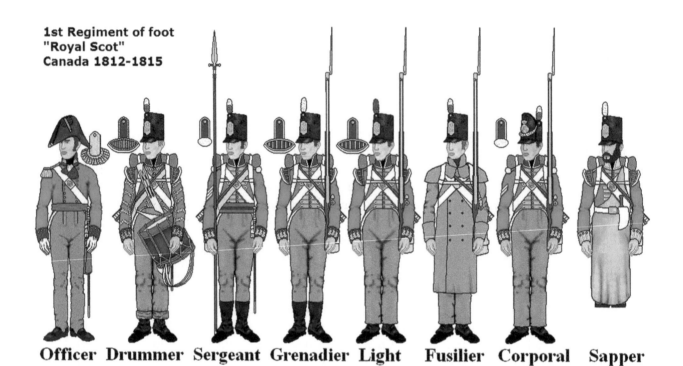

1st Regiment of foot "Royal Scot" Canada 1812-1815

Officer   Drummer   Sergeant   Grenadier   Light infantryman   Fusilier   Corporal   Sapper

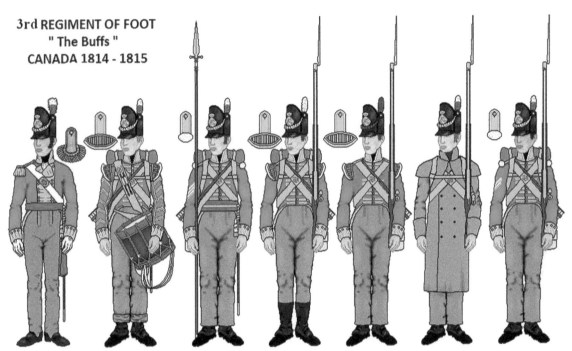

3rd REGIMENT OF FOOT
" The Buffs "
CANADA 1814 - 1815

Captain   Drummer   Sergeant   Grenadier   Light   Fusilier   Corporal
infantryman

4th REGIMENT OF FOOT
CANADA 1814 - 1815

Captain Drummer Sergeant Grenadier Light Fusilier Corporal
infantryman

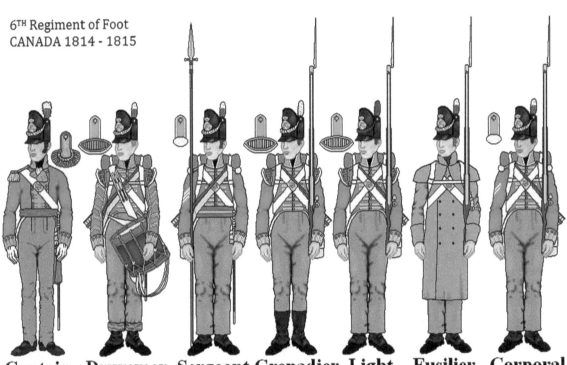

6TH Regiment of Foot
CANADA 1814 - 1815

Captain   **Drummer**   **Sergeant**   **Grenadier**   **Light infantryman**   **Fusilier**   **Corporal**

7th REGIMENT OF FOOT
"ROYAL FUSILIERS"

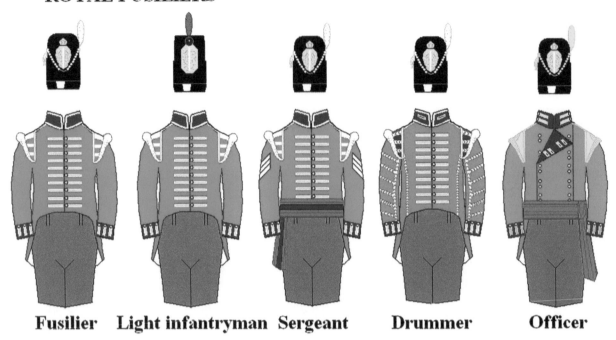

Fusilier **Light infantryman** **Sergeant** **Drummer** **Officer**

21st REGIMENT OF FOOT
"ROYAL NORTH BRITISH FUSILIERS"

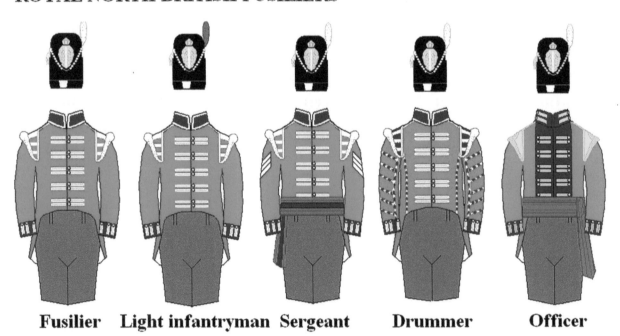

Fusilier **Light infantryman** **Sergeant** **Drummer** **Officer**

41st REGIMENT OF FOOT
CANADA 1812 - 1815

Captain   **Drummer**   **Sergeant**   **Grenadier**   **Light infantrymen**   **Corporal**

44th REGIMENT OF FOOT "ESSEX"

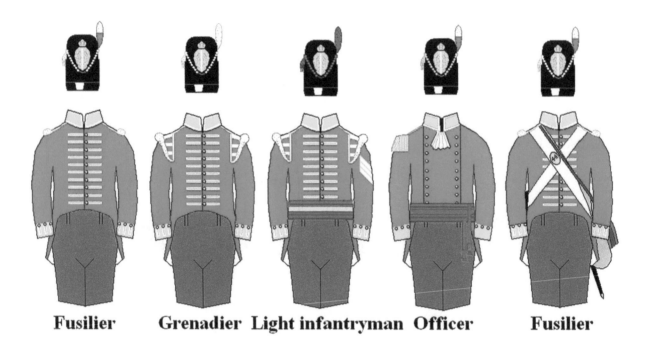

Fusilier   Grenadier   Light infantryman   Officer   Fusilier

89th REGIMENT OF FOOT

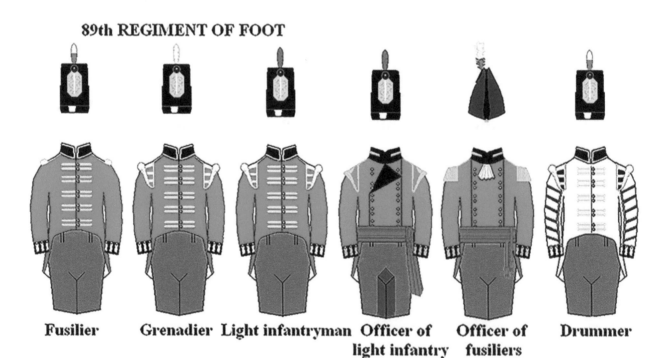

Fusilier   Grenadier   Light infantryman   Officer of   Officer of   Drummer
light infantry   fusiliers

49th REGIMENT OF FOOT

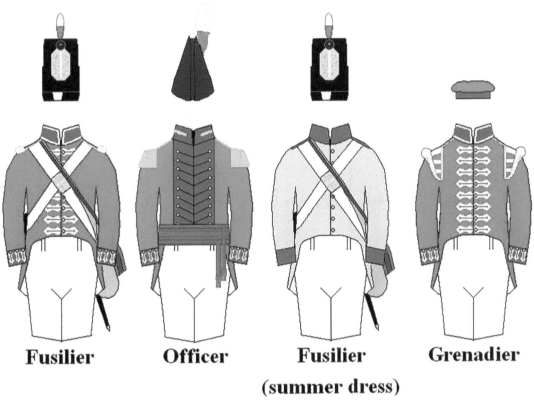

Fusilier   **Officer**   **Fusilier**   **Grenadier**

(summer dress)

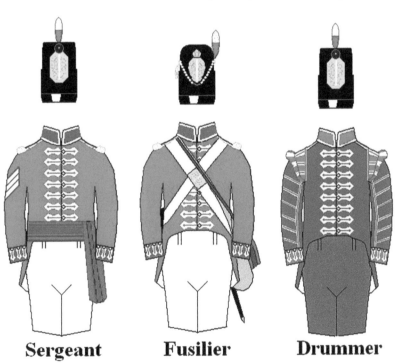

Sergeant   **Fusilier**   **Drummer**

93rd Regiment of foot 1814 -1815
"SUTHERLAND HIGHLANDERS"

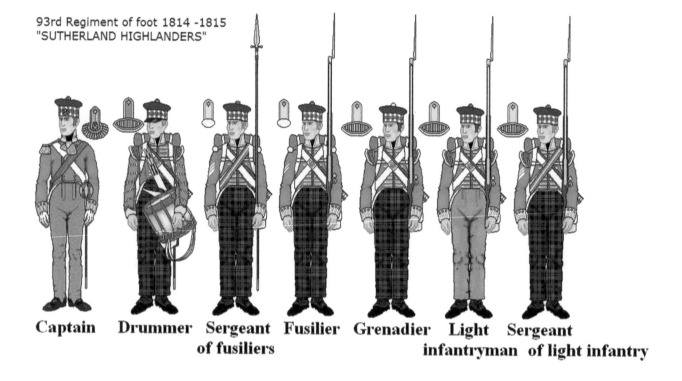

Captain   **Drummer**   **Sergeant**   **Fusilier**   **Grenadier**   **Light**   **Sergeant**
of fusiliers   infantryman   of light infantry

100th REGIMENT OF FOOT

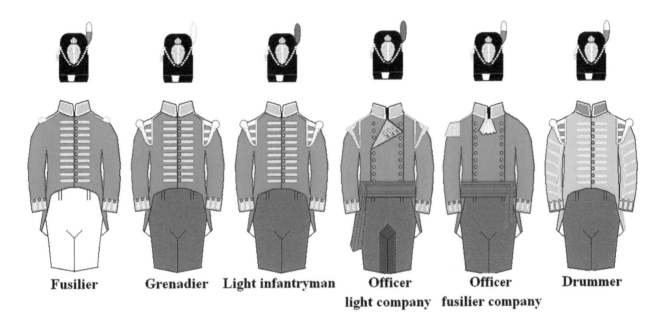

Fusilier   Grenadier   Light infantryman   Officer
light company   Officer
fusilier company   Drummer

104th FOOT
New-Brunswick Reg
CANADA 1810-1817

Officer Trumpeter Sergeant Grenadier Light infantrymen Corporal Sapper

10th ROYAL VETERAN BATTALION 1812-1815

Officer   Drummer   Sergeant   Soldiers

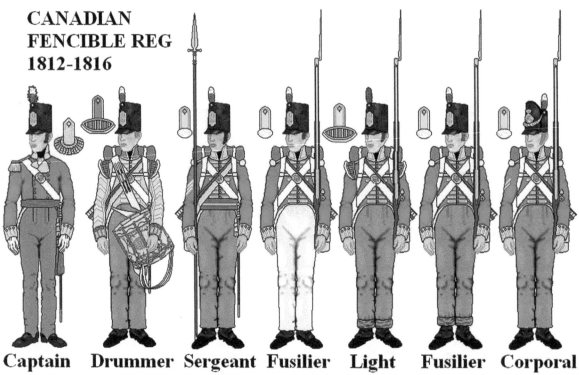

CANADIAN FENCIBLE REG 1812-1816

Captain　　Drummer　Sergeant　Fusilier　Light infantryman　Fusilier　Corporal

Independent Companies of Foreigners

Soldiers

Rifles and light infantry

Due to the heavy military involvement in the wars against Napoleon, Britain was not able to send major reinforcements to Canada during 1812 and 1813; it was only in 1814, with the temporary defeat and exile of the French Emperor, that the Crown could send more regular and veteran regiments to fight against the Americans. Among the reinforcements sent to North America there were the famous "Rifles" and a few cavalry units. After Braddock's disastrous defeat in 1755 (during the French-Indian War), the British Army understood that it was absolutely necessary to have an independent unit of light infantrymen (equipped with rifled weapons) for service in North America. As a result, the 62nd "Royal American" Regiment was formed in 1756 with volunteers coming from the Thirteen Colonies. The new corps was mainly formed to fight against the native American and Canadian raiders who were backed by France, since they were real masters of bush fighting and thus could not be effectively countered by the line infantry regiments of redcoats. The new regiment was to act as the core of the British garrison in North America and was to comprise volunteers with different backgrounds in order to become an elite colonial unit; the early volunteers of this corps, in fact, had different ethnic origins: there were German and Swiss experienced veterans who had already served in their countries as light infantrymen, as well as local American colonists and British elite soldiers coming from other regular regiments at the service of the Crown. In February 1757 the unit was renamed as the 60th "Royal American" Regiment and with this new denomination it took part to several important engagements of the French-Indian War. Very soon the soldiers of the "Royal American" demonstrated to be excellent light infantrymen and learned all the specific tactics of forest warfare; as a result, the British reduced their original gap with the irregular military forces of the natives and Canadian "voyageurs". During the American Revolution the "Royal American" Regiment remained loyal to the Crown and fought with great valour against the patriots of the southern Thirteen Colonies.

When the Napoleonic Wars broke out, the 60th was deployed in Europe in order to fight against the French; by 1812 the regiment comprised a total of six battalions: four of light infantrymen and two of "rifles". Since the North American theatre of war against the US needed more light infantry units, the British authorities decided to expand the 60th Regiment by adding a further 7th Battalion that was specifically created for service in Canada. This battalion arrived in North America during April 1814 and soon took part to some of the major military engagements of the following months. It comprised six companies that were equipped with the light version of the standard Brown Bess musket and two companies that were armed with rifled Baker carbines. Most of its members, continuing the peculiar tradition of the regiment, were foreigners (volunteers coming from Germany and Switzerland as well as ex-prisoners of war coming from France or the Netherlands). This unit, however, was not the only corps of rifles sent to Canada by the British during 1812-1815. In 1800, bearing in mind the successes of the 60th "Royal American Regiment", the Crown formed an "Experimental Corps of Riflemen" that was to be completely equipped with the formidable Baker rifled carbine. The unit was created by assembling chosen volunteers who came from various infantry regiments of the British Army; in 1802 the "provisional" corps of riflemen was officially made part of the regular infantry as the "95th Regiment of Foot". Being formed by three battalions, the Rifle Regiment soon became one of the best infantry unit of the whole British Army: divided into several detachments, it took part to all the most important campaigns and expeditions that were organized by the Crown against Napoleon. In 1815, for the British campaign against New Orleans, the 3rd Battalion of the 95th "Rifles" was transferred to the North American theatre of operations. At the Battle of New Orleans, the elite riflemen fought with great valour, but could do nothing to avoid the British defeat. Before 1808, in addition to the 60th and 95th Regiments, the British Army included also other units of light infantry that could fight like line units. They were, however, proper light infantry and not a regiment of rifles (its men were armed with the light version of the smoothbore Brown Bess musket). After fighting against the excellent French light infantry during the Peninsular War, the British decided to transform several of their existing line infantry regiments into light units. By 1812 the following regiments were converted: 51st, 52nd, 68th, 71st and 85th Regiments of Foot. All these had the same internal structure that was standard for the line infantry, but the companies of their battalions were all light ones (there were no fusiliers and grenadiers).

85th foot
1814-1815

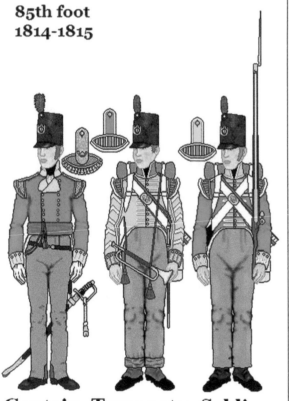

Captain Trumpeter Soldier

43rd foot
1814-1815

Captain Trumpeter Soldier

60th Regiment of Rifles
" Royal American "
1814-1815
7th Battalion

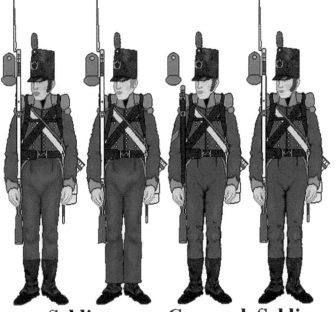

Captain Trumpeter Sergeant   Soldiers   Corporal Soldier

Cavalry and Technical Corps

As we already said, the British reinforcements sent to Canada included also some cavalry units. The first two were the 14th and 19th Regiments of Light Dragoons; as usual, light corps were the chosen one for service on the broken terrain of North America. The 14th Light Dragoons only took part in the campaign of New Orleans but arrived in America without horses and thus the majority of its members fought dismounted. The 19th Light Dragoons, instead, arrived with all its horses in Canada during 1813. This is different from the 14th Regiment, which only sent part of its soldiers to North America, the 19th Regiment was sent to Canada with all its three squadrons. The 19th Regiment of Light Dragoons was never used as a consolidated regiment during the war, since two of its squadrons were deployed in Upper Canada and the remaining one in Lower Canada. The few light dragoons were attached to each military contingent and employed as scouts, escorts and couriers: they rarely performed as "shock" cavalry. The last cavalry unit of the British Army to be involved in the War of 1812 was the 6th Regiment of Heavy Dragoons ("Inniskilling", an Irish regiment): during the Chesapeake Campaign of 1814, in fact, this corps provided a small detachment of a few men to provide a mounted escort for the British general staff.

In 1812 the Royal Artillery was made up of a total of ten foot battalions, each with ten companies; a company corresponded to a battery and the latter generally comprised six artillery pieces (usually five field guns of the same calibre and a single howitzer). Rocket launchers were also quite popular, being used on several occasions during the conflict. At the beginning of the war with the US there were nine companies of Royal Artillery in Canada, each named after its commander: one company from the 2nd Battalion, four companies from the 4th Battalion, one company from the 5th Battalion, one company from the 6th Battalion and one company from the 7th Battalion. In 1814 another six companies of foot artillery were sent to Canada: one from the 1st Battalion, one from the 4th Battalion, one from the 5th Battalion, one from the 9th Battalion and two from the 10th Battalion. The British technical corps obviously comprised also the Royal Engineers and the Royal Military Artificers/Royal Sappers and Miners. The Engineer corps deployed only 23 officers in Canada, while the artificers/sappers and miners were mostly provided by the local Canadian contingents (since the British component of these corps was extremely scarce).

14th LIGHT DRAGOONS
1814-1815

Officer   Trumpeter Sergeant   Soldiers   Corporal

19th LIGHT DRAGOONS
1814-1815

Officer Trumpeter Sergeant   Soldiers   Corporal

6th "INNISKILLING" DRAGOONS

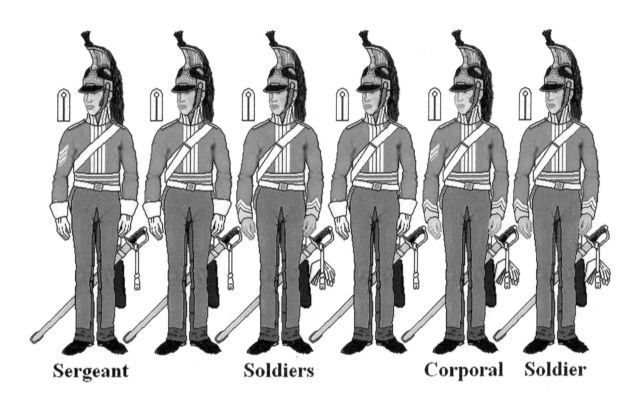

Sergeant　　　　**Soldiers**　　　　**Corporal**　**Soldier**

ROYAL ARTILLERY

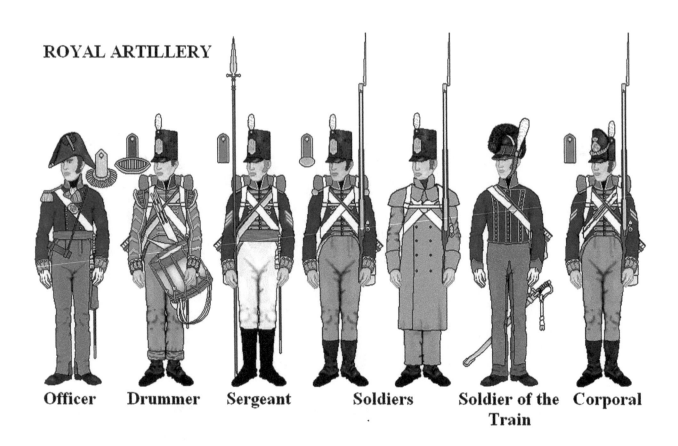

Officer   Drummer   Sergeant   Soldiers   Soldier of the   Corporal
                                                               Train

ROYAL ENGINEERS, ROYAL SAPPERS AND MINERS

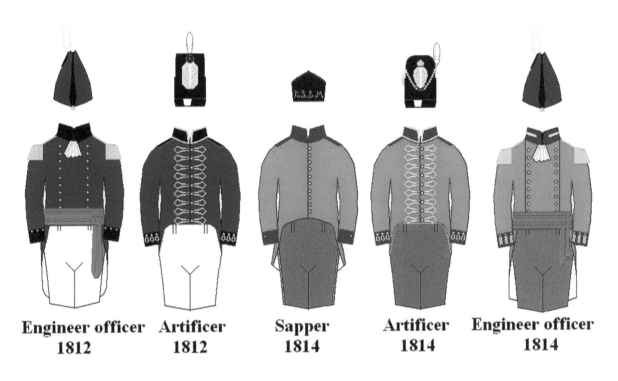

Engineer officer
1812

Artificer
1812

Sapper
1814

Artificer
1814

Engineer officer
1814

Foreign and colonial units

During the War of 1812 against the USA, Britain deployed two Swiss regiments of infantry in Canada: "De Watteville" Regiment and "De Meuron" Regiment. The first was formed in 1801, by assembling the remaining officers and soldiers of six Swiss mercenary regiments that had served in the Austrian Army against Napoleon (which had been paid by the British). After fighting for years in the Mediterranean, the "De Watteville" Regiment was transferred to Canada in April 1813. The unit was finally disbanded on 24 October 1816 and its former members received some grants of land in Canada. The Regiment "De Meuron" was originally raised in 1781 for service with the Dutch East India Company; in 1796, while at garrison in Ceylon, the unit passed into British service. After taking part to several military campaigns in India, it was transferred to the Mediterranean and then to the Iberian Peninsula in order to fight against the French; on 5 May 1813 it was sent to Canada. Like the "De Watteville" Regiment, this Swiss unit also fought with great distinction against the Americans on several occasions. Disbanded in 1816, most of its former members received some grants of land in Canada. Both these elite Swiss units had the same standard establishment of a British line infantry regiment.

In 1795 the British formed eight colonial infantry regiments in their possessions of the Caribbean (the West Indies); these were mostly formed with free blacks and with slaves who were purchased from the local plantations. In 1798 another five of such units were created (bringing the total to 12), but during 1802-1803 five of the regiments were disbanded (three in 1802 and two in 1803). In 1807 all the slaves who had been purchased for service in the "West India Regiments" were freed by the British government. Officers and NCOs of these units were all whites. The soldiers from these regiments were extremely valuable for the British Army, since they were the only who could operate efficiently in the difficult climatic conditions of the Caribbean (where the hot weather and tropical diseases caused hundreds of deaths among European white soldiers). During the War of 1812 the 1st, 2nd and 5th "West India Regiments" were employed at various times against the Americans. Despite being defined as "regiments", these units had the establishment and internal structure of a standard British line infantry battalion. By 1815 only seven of such regiments remained in British service, being later reduced to two (one regiment was disbanded in 1816, two in 1817 and two in 1819).

REGIMENT De WATTEVILLE
CANADA   1813-1816

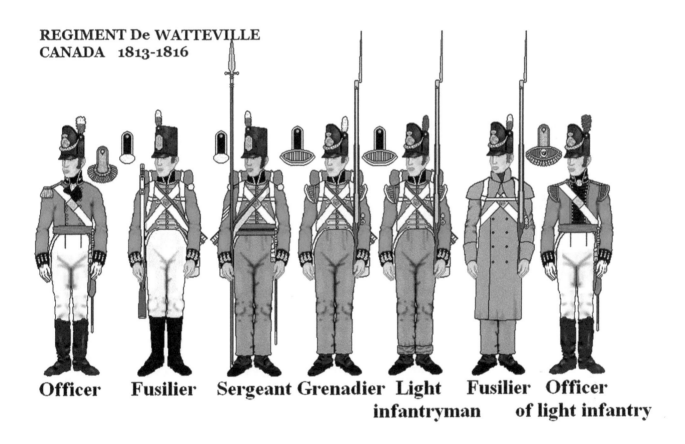

Officer   Fusilier   Sergeant Grenadier Light   Fusilier Officer
infantryman   of light infantry

REGIMENT De MEURON
CANADA 1813-1816

Captain Drummer Sergeant Grenadier Light Fusilier Corporal
infantryman

1st, 2nd, 5th WEST INDIA REGIMENTS
1812- 1815

Fusilier 1st REG Fusilier 5th REG Officer 1st REG Grenadier 5th REG Fusilier 2nd REG Fusilier 5th REG Sergeant 2nd REG

The Royal Marines and Royal Marine Artillery

During the last phase of the war, the British military forces in North America could also count on the support of the elite Royal Marines. They operated as naval infantry on the British warships but were frequently employed also as "shock" troops during the frequent raids that were launched against the American coastline on the Atlantic. Up to 1810 the Royal Marines had been organized in independent companies, with 30,000 men in total, which were placed on the various warships of the Royal Navy. In that year, however, a 1st Battalion of Royal Marines (a permanent unit) was formed by assembling six companies; a 2nd Battalion was created in July 1812, always with six companies; a 3rd Battalion was added on 21 January 1814, having ten companies. The 1st and 2nd Battalions arrived in North America during June 1813, while the 3rd one was sent to fight against the Americans only in late June 1814. In May 1814, shortly before the arrival of the new 3rd Battalion, the 2nd one was broken up and its remaining men were assigned to other functions. As a result, the former 3rd Battalion soon became the new 2nd one and a new 3rd Battalion was formed by assembling two existing units of "Colonial Marines". The "First Corps of Colonial Marines" was formed in 1808, while the "Second Corps of Colonial Marines" was raised in 1814; both units were made up of free blacks (former slaves) who came from the British possessions in the Caribbean. Since most of the regular "Royal Marines" were involved into the military operations taking place in Europe, the British decided to raise some locals for service on their warships operating in the Caribbean. The regular battalions of Royal Marines serving in North America were supported by some companies of the Royal Marine Artillery, a naval artillery corps that was formed in 1804 to support the Marines embarked on warships. Each of the three battalions had an attached company of Royal Marine Artillery. Already before the outbreak of the war with the US, the sailors manning the military vessels on the Great Lakes (Ontario, Erie and Huron) had been organized into a small colonial corps simply known as "Provincial Marine"; on 24 June 1813, however, this unit was transferred from the competence of the local colonial authorities to that of the Royal Navy. During the war, some sailors serving on the warships of the Royal Navy were transferred to the "Provincial Marine" for the naval operations conducted on the Great Lakes.

ROYAL MARINES

Officer   Soldiers   Drummer   Colonial   Sergeant   Royal
Marine   Marine Artillery

Royal Marines

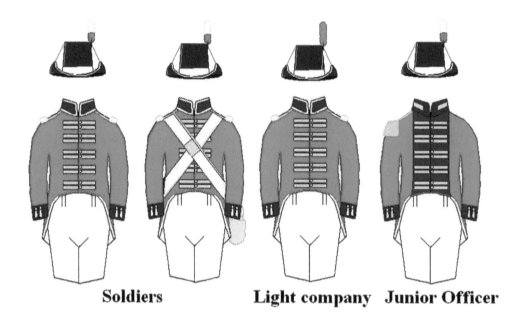

Soldiers   **Light company**   **Junior Officer**

COLONIAL MARINES

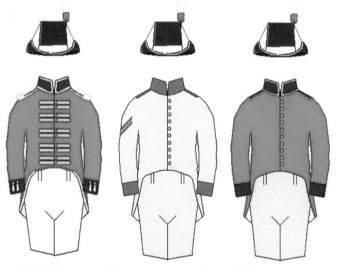

Full dress   **Summer service dress**   **Winter service dress**

Royal Marine Artillery

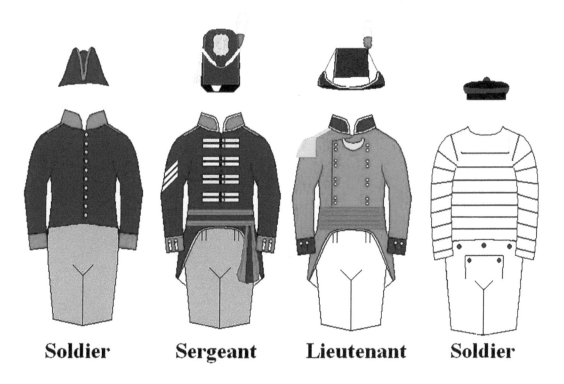

Soldier   **Sergeant**   **Lieutenant**   **Soldier**

Chapter 5: Canadian Militia and Volunteers From 1812 to 1815

In Canada, like in the USA by way of England, the militia was formed by all the able-bodied men who were eligible for military service according to their age. Since the foundation of the first French settlements, in the early decades of the 17th century, the Canadians had to adopt a form of local military organization in order to repulse the violent raids of the various native tribes. This system was implemented during the 18th century and saw the Canadian militiamen fighting with great valour against the British and their native allies during the French-Indian War. In contrast with what was seen in the Thirteen Colonies, the militia units of French Canada were under a quite strict control from the central authorities of the colony. The Canadian militia had fewer men than their American equivalents, but their members were individuals with strong military capabilities. Most of the settlers living in Canada outside of the cities were huntsmen and thus were used to travel long distances with the worst weather conditions. They had an expert knowledge of the vast forests and plains surrounding them and were all excellent marksmen (employing many long and rifled muskets exactly like the American colonists).

Thanks to their high mobility and great capacity to organize ambushes, the Canadian militiamen were able to fight against the northern tribes on almost equal terms. They had a strong and intimate knowledge of the enemy's guerrilla warfare and thus could launch surprise attacks as needed. The Canadian militia could also be used during winter and had all the needed equipment to survive extremely cold temperatures. Rivers and lakes were not real barriers for them, since the use of canoes was extremely common. In general, albeit being quite few if compared with their American opponents, the Canadian militiamen were excellent soldiers. The British inherited the militia system from the French and did nothing to change it; instead, they tried to "regularize" as much as possible the Canadian militia units in order to transform them into a proper "auxiliary army" that could support the regular forces (something that George Washington tried to do in the US, but without success). Much of Canada's north-eastern population consisted of French settlers, who had always been extremely loyal to France until the very last days of the French-Indian War. As a result, at the outbreak of the war in 1812, the British authorities feared that these men could refuse to serve in the militia or revolt against the Crown.

The Canadian colonists, instead, all remained loyal to Britain with no distinctions existing between the Francophone and Anglophone ones. The Canadians already considered their territories as a "nation" and thus the foreign aggression of the US did nothing else than augmenting their patriotic feelings. From 1791 the territory of Canada was divided in two provinces: Lower

Canada and Upper Canada; in addition to these there were also the so-called "Indian Territory" and the smaller "Atlantic Colonies": the first comprised all the unsettled lands that were located west of the Great Lakes, while the second were formed by the smaller British colonies that were situated on the Atlantic coast (Nova Scotia, New Brunswick, Newfoundland, Prince Edward Island and Cape Breton Island). For practical reasons, we will describe the organization of the Canadian militia and volunteers in separate paragraphs for each of the above territories.

Militia and volunteers of Lower Canada

The province of Lower Canada corresponded to the former territory of "New France" and thus comprised most of the Francophone settlers living in British North America. It had a much larger population than Upper Canada and comprised the three most important cities of British North America: Québec, Montréal and Trois-Rivières. The militia of this colony, similarly to what happened in the American states, comprised an active force (known as "Select Militia") and a reserve one (known as "Sedentary Militia"). The former was activated only in case of foreign menace and consisted of the best elements coming from the general "Sedentary Militia". When a unit was called to serve, no matter if coming from the "Select Militia" or from the "Sedentary" one, it received the further title of "Embodied" (which meant "attached to the regulars"). In February 1812, as part of the mobilization in view of the war with the US, a total of 6,500 militiamen were activated to form the "Select Embodied Militia" of Lower Canada. They were initially structured on four infantry battalions with 800 men each, which were to serve for a period of two years. After war was declared, a 5th Battalion was added on 21 September; in late June 1813 the flank companies of the five existing units were assembled together in order to form two independent battalions of light infantry, called "Militia Light Infantry Battalions".

The Militia Light Battalions were temporary units and thus were dissolved on 25 November 1813 (with the various companies returning to their original battalions). A 6th Battalion was formed on 28 February 1813 and briefly served as garrison of Quebec; this had a smaller establishment if compared with the existing ones and was disbanded in September 1814. In March 1814 the 5th Battalion was reorganized as an independent light infantry unit and received the denomination of "Canadian Chasseurs" (see below). The original four units continued to serve with distinction until the end of the war, being discharged only on 1 March 1815. The "Select Militia" of Lower Canada comprised also the following units:

Canadian Voltiguers: this unit was raised in April 1812, during the pre-war mobilization. It was an elite corps of light infantry, which soon became legendary because of its great achievements during the conflict. As clear from its denomination, it was entirely made up of Francophone colonists and consisted of a single battalion with more or less 550 soldiers. Dispersed in various small detachments that were attached to several major military units, the "Voltiguers Canadiens" fought as scouts and skirmishers with enormous valour (especially during the early phases of the American invasion).

Compagnie des Guides: this was a small cavalry unit, also known as "Corps of Guides". Formed in September 1812, it comprised just 2 officers and 30 troopers.

Royal Militia Artillery: this consisted of just 1 officer and 22 gunners, who were detached from the urban militia of Montréal during September 1812 in order to be absorbed into the "Select Embodied Militia".

Corps of Canadian Voyageurs: this was a rather unusual corps raised by the North-West Fur Company, which operated in the vast areas located around Hudson Bay. The "Voyageurs" were the Canadian equivalent of American "trappers", being frontier huntsmen who lived a very solitary life in the woods of North America. The "Corps of Canadian Voyageurs" was formed by the same North-West Fur Company with a certain number of its employees. This unit was created in October 1812 having as main objective that of militarizing the "voyageurs" and transforming them into proper soldiers. These men played a crucial role during the war, since their first responsibility was that of protecting the supplies which moved from the city of Montréal to the western outposts of the Indian Territory. On 14 March 1813, after becoming famous for the scarce discipline of its members, the unit was finally disbanded.

Québec Volunteers: this unit was raised in Québec City during November 1812, being made up of a single infantry battalion with six companies. Initially the battalion was to have also an attached battery of artillery, but this was never formed. On 13 February 1813 the "Québec Volunteers" were absorbed into the new 6th Battalion of "Select Embodied Militia".

Corps of Provincial Royal Artillery Drivers: formed during April 1813, this small corps was attached to the regular detachments of the Royal Artillery that were operating in the Montréal District. The local Canadians had to provide drivers for the batteries of the regular artillery, since most of the British artillerymen were employed as gunners and not for "auxiliary" duties. Canadian Light Dragoons: recruited in the Montréal District during the spring of 1813, this small cavalry corps comprised just 80 men (assembled into a single troop). The unit saw much action and took part to several engagements, being finally disbanded only in May 1815.

Dorchester Provincial Light Dragoons: raised during the spring of 1813 like the "Canadian Light Dragoons", also this corps was a small cavalry unit. It consisted of a single troop with 68 men, who were armed and equipped by the government but had to buy horses and uniforms at their own expense. The "Dorchester Provincial Light Dragoons" served in Québec until being disbanded in March 1815.

Provincial Commissariat Voyageurs: this unit was formed on 8 April 1813, to act as a replacement for the recently disbanded "Corps of Canadian Voyageurs". The new corps continued the activities of the previous one but with a higher level of efficiency and discipline. It consisted of one captain, ten lieutenants, ten sergeants and 400 rankers.

Frontier Light Infantry: this small corps consisted of just two companies and was created to patrol the American border south of Montréal. On 13 August 1813, after less than three months of existence, it was attached to the "Canadian Voltigeurs"; the two companies of the "Frontier Light Infantry" became the 9th and 10th Companies of the famous Francophone unit.

Independent Company of Militia Volunteers: created in May 1813, this unit was soon attached to the "Frontier Light Infantry". Some months later, in February 1814, the "Independent Company of Militia Volunteers" was completely absorbed into the "Frontier Light Infantry".

Canadian Chasseurs: as we have already seen, this unit was the ex-5th Battalion of the "Select Embodied Militia". With its new denomination it was usually brigaded with the "Canadian Voltiguers" and "Frontier Light Infantry". In total the "Canadian Chasseurs" had just six companies. The unit was disbanded on 24 March 1815.

Since it was directly menaced by the American invasion, Lower Canada mobilized its "Sedentary Militia". This numbered around 54,000 militiamen, which were organized in two different ways according to their ethnic origins. The "Sedentary Militia" of the Francophone communities had the "parish company" as basic unit: each parish (generally corresponding to a village) was to provide an infantry company commanded by a captain. The various "parish companies" were assembled into three "divisions", which had the same numerical establishment of a regiment. Each of the three districts that made up the province of Lower Canada (Québec, Montréal and Trois-Rivières) had one of these "divisions". The few Anglophone settlers of Lower Canada had a different military organization: they lived in the so-called "Eastern Townships", which had been settled by Loyalist colonists during the American Revolution, and thus formed an independent district. The "Eastern Townships" District had a militia that was organized according to counties, in perfect English style. Each county, according to its population, was to provide one or more infantry regiments with six battalions each. The single battalions could sometimes have an attached troop of cavalry. The one described above was the general organization of the "Sedentary Militia" in rural areas; in the major cities of Québec, Montréal and Trois-Rivières the situation was completely different. These important centres, in fact, had several infantry battalions of "urban" militiamen. Québec had three infantry battalions: the 1st and 2nd were made up of Francophone citizens, while the 3rd one comprised Anglophone militiamen; Montréal also had three infantry battalions: the first was made up of Anglophone citizens, while the second and third ones comprised Francophone militiamen. Québec's battalions (created in 1803) had "flank" companies like those of the regular military forces; these were made up of volunteers and not of standard militiamen. The battalions from Montréal had "flank" companies, which were assembled for some time in order to form a temporary "elite" battalion. The "urban" militias of Québec and Montréal also raised one troop of cavalry and two companies of artillery each, which were all formed with well-educated volunteers. The "urban" militia of Trois-Rivières consisted of a single infantry battalion. The "urban" militias took part to no significant military actions during the war and were disbanded as soon as the American menace vanished in 1815.

SEDENTARY MILITIA OF LOWER CANADA

Officer   **Voyageur**   **Militiamen**

SEDENTARY MILITIA OF LOWER CANADA

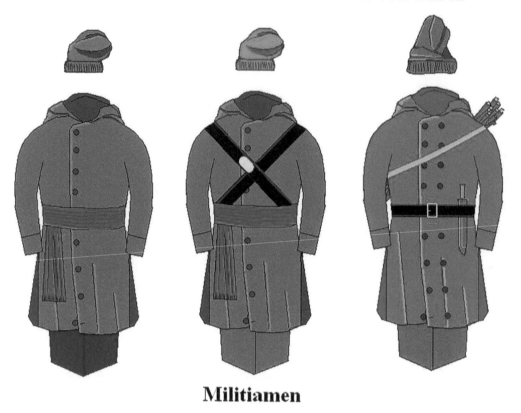

Militiamen

CANADIAN VOLTIGEURS

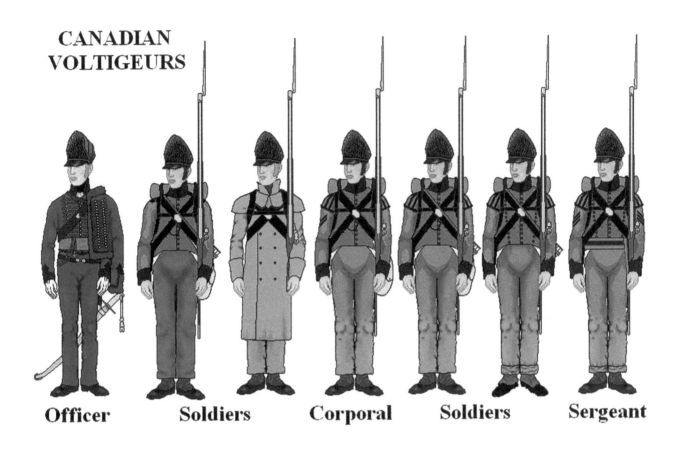

Officer   **Soldiers**   **Corporal**   **Soldiers**   **Sergeant**

CANADIAN VOYAGEURS

Winter dress   **Summer dress**

PROVINCIAL VOYAGEURS

Voyageurs   **Officer**

INDEPENDENT LIGHT INFANTRY UNITS
OF LOWER CANADA

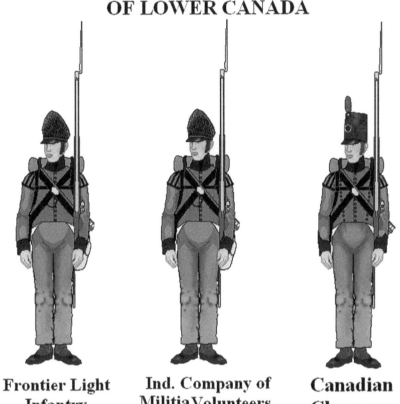

**Frontier Light
Infantry**

**Ind. Company of
Militia Volunteers**

**Canadian
Chasseurs**

Company of Guides

Canadian Light Dragoons

Urban militia of Quebec

Dorchester Provincial Light Dragoons

Urban militia of Montréal

MILITIA ARTILLERY OF LOWER AND UPPER CANADA

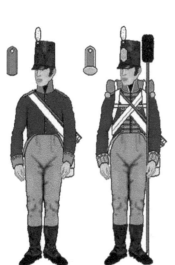

Urban militia of Montréal

Incorporated artillery company

Upper Canada

Provincial Royal Artillery Drivers

Upper Canada

Artilleryman of Sedentary Militia

Upper Canada

URBAN MILITIA AND VOLUNTEERS OF QUEBEC

URBAN MILITIA

VOLUNTEERS

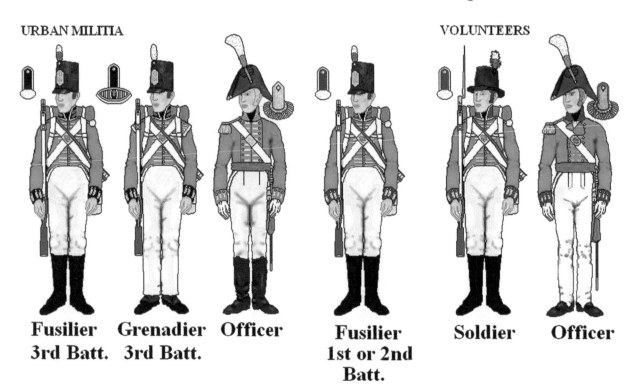

**Fusilier
3rd Batt.**

**Grenadier
3rd Batt.**

Officer

**Fusilier
1st or 2nd
Batt.**

Soldier

Officer

URBAN MILITIAS OF MONTREAL AND TROIS-RIVIERES

MONTREAL

TROIS-RIVIERES

Soldier
2nd/3rd
Batt.
1812

Soldier
1st
Batt.
1812

Soldier
2nd/3rd
Batt.
1813

Flank company
2nd/3rd
Batt.
1813

Officer
2nd/3rd
Batt.
1813

Officer
2nd/3rd
Batt.
1814

Soldier

Officer

Militia and volunteers of Upper Canada

The province of Upper Canada had been mostly inhabited, at least initially, by Loyalist Americans who abandoned the Thirteen Colonies during the Revolution against Britain. It saw much of the combat operations of the 1812-1815 war taking place on its territory and thus suffered a lot from the devastations caused by the battling armies. Despite having a smaller population than Lower Canada, the province of Upper Canada gave a significant contribution to the British war effort. From a geographical point of view, Upper Canada comprised the vast territory located between the western border of Quebec province and the city of Windsor on Lake Huron. In total, the province comprised eight districts divided into several counties. The "Sedentary Militia" of Upper Canada was much younger than that of Lower Canada, having been organized for the first time in 1793. Similarly, to what happened in the "Eastern Townships" District of Lower Canada, it was based on county regiments of infantry that consisted of a single battalion with ten companies. In March 1812, some months before the outbreak of the war with the US, each battalion was enlarged with the addition of two "flank" companies; the latter were made up of volunteers, all having less than 40 years of age. On 18 March 1813, a single battalion of "Select Embodied Militia" with ten companies was formed in Upper Canada; in total it comprised around 500 men, the best elements of the "Sedentary Militia". The companies of this single battalion took part to several important engagements of the war and demonstrated to be units of high quality (comparable to that of the British regular units). In addition to the above, the province of Upper Canada deployed also the following independent corps:

Glengarry Light Infantry: on 13 February 1812, even before the declaration of war, the "Glengarry Light Infantry" was created from Scottish settlers who lived in eastern Upper Canada. Since most of this battalion's members came from the same areas of Scotland, the "Glengarry Light Infantry" was characterised by a strong esprit-de-corps that made it an elite unit. The 730 soldiers of this corps were organized into eight companies, which were all light ones: the members of the "Glengarry Light Infantry", in fact, all underwent intensive light infantry training and were equipped exactly as the famous "Rifle Regiment" of the regular British Army. The soldiers of this corps proved to be excellent marksmen and took part to many important actions of the war against the US; the "Glengarry Light Infantry" was finally disbanded in 1816, after having gained deep respect from its enemies.

Volunteers of 1812: as we have already seen, the infantry battalions of the "Sedentary Militia" were expanded with the creation of volunteer "flank" companies; in order to face the American invasion, however, the volunteers of Upper Canada formed also some independent corps that became known as "Volunteers of 1812". These were named after their county of origin and comprised six companies of rifles, ten troops of cavalry and three companies of artillery. In addition, there was also one infantry company of free blacks, one company of naval infantry (formed for service on the Great Lakes) and one company of artillery drivers.

Provincial Light Dragoons: these consisted of just three small corps, each formed in a different county of Upper Canada. The "Niagara Provincial Light Dragoons" were a troop of just 50 men, which was renamed as "Niagara Frontier Guides" on 24 October 1814. The other two troops were created in April 1813 and later assembled into a single unit.

Incorporated Artillery Company: raised in March 1813, it comprised both artillerymen and artillery drivers who were absorbed into the "Select Embodied Militia".

Provincial Royal Artillery Drivers: formed during January 1813, this small corps (two companies) was attached to the regular detachments of the Royal Artillery that were operating in Upper Canada. The local Canadians had to provide drivers for the batteries of the regular artillery, since most of the British artillerymen were employed as gunners and not for "auxiliary" duties.

Corps of Provincial Artificers: formed in March 1813 to assist the regular Royal Engineers operating in Upper Canada, this unit was also known as "Coloured Corps" because all its members were free blacks.

Caldwell's Rangers: also known as "Western Rangers", this corps had two companies and was created in April 1813. Members of this unit were to serve side by side with the native allies of Britain in Upper Canada; as a result, they were equipped as proper light infantry "rangers".

Loyal Kent Volunteers: a single company of volunteer militiamen, formed on 25 November 1813 in Kent County. It was later attached to the battalion of "Select Embodied Militia".

Loyal London Volunteers: a single company of volunteer militiamen, formed on 24 November 1813 in the small town of London (Upper Canada). Disbanded on 24 February 1814.

Loyal Essex Volunteers: a single company of volunteer militiamen, formed during March 1814 in Essex County. Being also known as "Essex Rangers", it was disbanded on 24 March 1815.

SEDENTARY MILITIA OF UPPER CANADA

1812

1813

Officer

Militiamen

Militiamen

SEDENTARY MILITIA OF UPPER CANADA 1814-1815

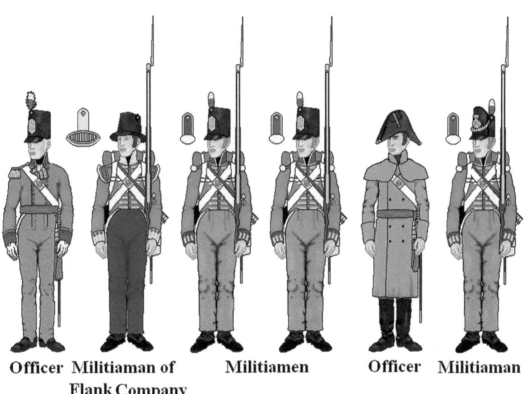

Officer   Militiaman of   Militiamen   Officer   Militiaman
Flank Company

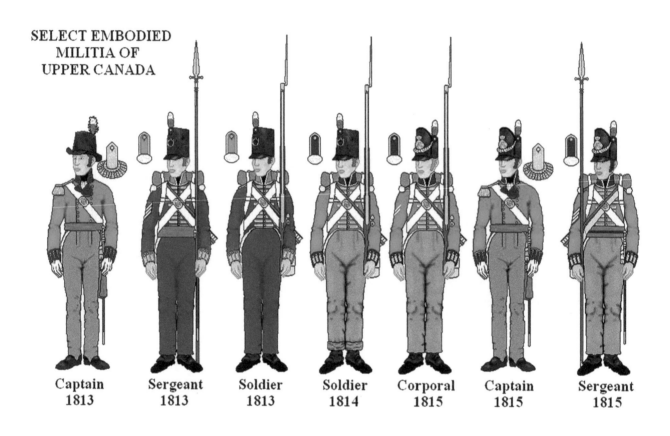

SELECT EMBODIED
MILITIA OF
UPPER CANADA

Captain
1813

Sergeant
1813

Soldier
1813

Soldier
1814

Corporal
1815

Captain
1815

Sergeant
1815

GLENGARRY LIGHT INFANTRY

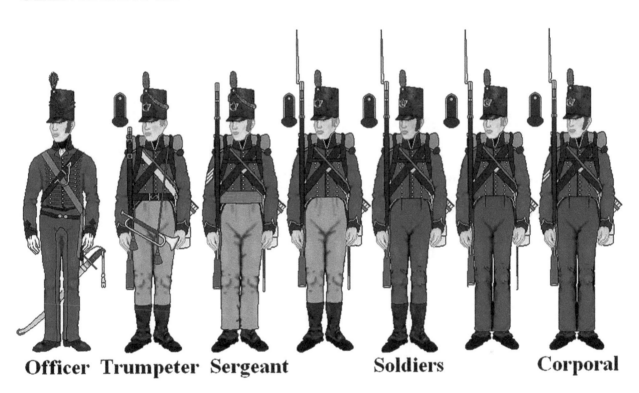

Officer Trumpeter Sergeant   Soldiers   Corporal

LEEDS

GLENGARRY

2nd Rifle Company

Officer   Soldier

**2nd
Rifle Company**

**1st
Rifle
Company**

DUNDAS

Volunteers

PROVINCIAL LIGHT DRAGOONS OF UPPER CANADA

Troopers

CALDWELL'S RANGERS

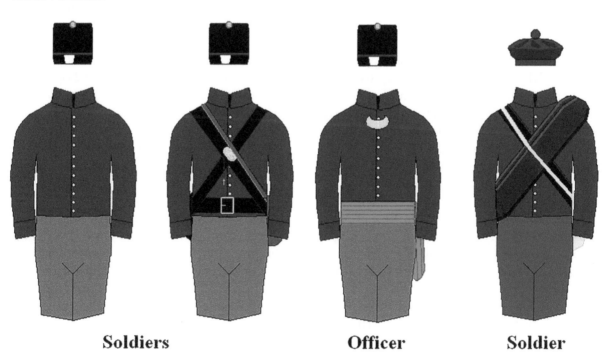

Soldiers   **Officer**   **Soldier**

Militia and Volunteers of the Native Territory and Atlantic Colonies

Indian Territory: since this region was mostly unsettled, being defended by just a few forts, very few military units were raised from it. The only "inhabitants" of the Indian Territory were "voyageurs" (hunters) and fur traders, who were partly "regularized" in order to serve in proper military corps. Coming from the upper Mississippi Valley, the British/Canadian forces were able to capture northern Michigan and Wisconsin from the Americans and kept the initiative in this theatre of operations for most of the war. The first unit to be formed in the Indian Territory was the "Michigan Fencibles", a small infantry company of just 45 men that was created by recruiting "voyageurs" and fur traders. As the other units of "Fencibles", it was formed to garrison a specific area of territory: in fact, the "Michigan Fencibles" were garrisoned in the strategic position of Fort Mackinac. The corps was disbanded at the end of the conflict, on 28 June 1815. In July 1814, other Francophone "voyageurs" were recruited in the Indian Territory in order to form some volunteer companies: these became known as "Mississippi Volunteers" and initially consisted of just one company with 65 men. Apparently, this volunteer corps comprised also a small detachment of artillery.

Nova Scotia: the general militia of Nova Scotia consisted of 26 infantry battalions, known by the name of the county in which they were formed. At that time Nova Scotia had 12 counties, so each of them formed a certain number of infantry battalions according to its population. Some of the infantry battalions had attached artillery companies; in addition, since 1813, each of them was to have two additional companies (one of light infantry and one of rifles). During the conflict, a total of more or less 500 militiamen were "embodied" for active service (fearing naval incursions from the American fleet). The city of Halifax, the "capital" of Nova Scotia, deployed also one volunteer company of artillery.

New Brunswick: the general militia of New Brunswick was organized on county infantry battalions like that of Nova Scotia, albeit being smaller. In December 1812, to replace the local garrison of regulars that was transferred for service in Canada, 500 militiamen were "embodied" for active service. Saint John, the colony's capital, had one company of volunteer artillery.

Newfoundland: there were no militia units in this small colony, only a volunteer unit known as "Loyal Volunteers of Saint John"; this comprised five infantry companies and was later renamed as "Saint John's Volunteer Rangers". The corps was disbanded during summer of 1814.

Prince Edward Island: this colony had three infantry regiments of the militia and three volunteer infantry companies in its capital (the city of Charlottetown). Each militia regiment was formed in one of the three counties that made up the colony; each of the formers included a different number of battalions according to its population. The three volunteer companies of Charlottetown were named as follows: "Loyal Scottish Volunteers", "Royal Kent" and "Prince's Regent Volunteers".

Cape Breton Island: the local militia consisted of 20 infantry companies, each commanded by a captain and two lieutenants.

TRIBES OF THE OHIO TERRITORY

Warriors　　　　　　　　　　**Chief**

THE ATLANTIC COLONIES: NOVA SCOTIA

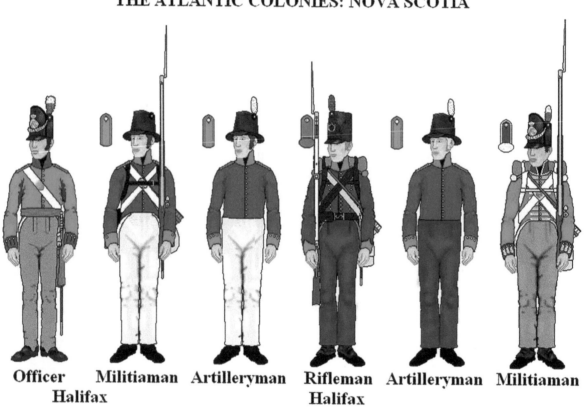

Officer
Halifax
Militiaman
Artilleryman
Rifleman
Halifax
Artilleryman
Militiaman

THE ATLANTIC COLONIES:
CAPE BRETON ISLAND AND NEW BRUNSWICK

Cape Breton Island

New Brunswick

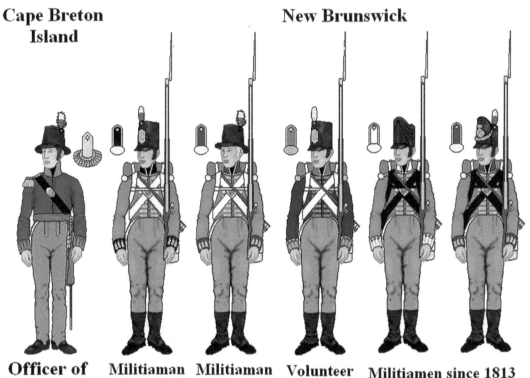

Officer of the Militia   **Militiaman York County**   **Militiaman Saint John**   **Volunteer Artillery of Saint John**   **Militiamen since 1813**

THE ATLANTIC COLONIES:
PRINCE EDWARD ISLAND AND NEWFOUNDLAND

Prince Edward Island

Newfoundland

Officer of Loyal Scottish Volunteers

Officer of Royal Kent

Militiaman

Saint John's Volunteer Rangers

Color Plates and Commentaries

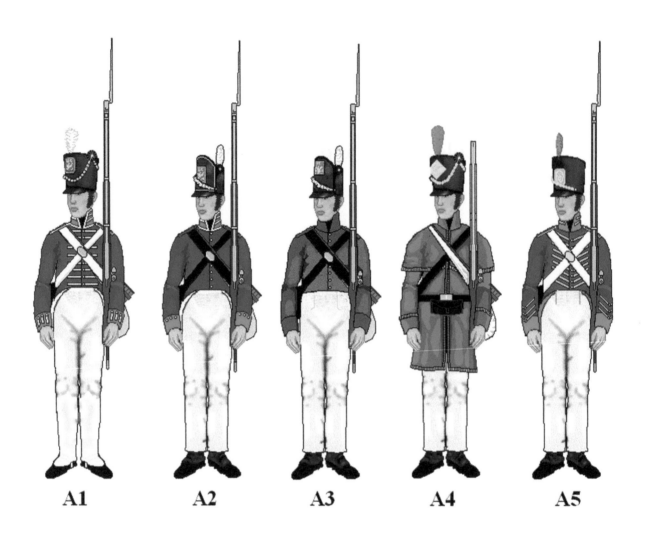

A1 **A2** **A3** **A4** **A5**

Plate A: US Line Infantry, Rifles and Marines

A1: Private, 16th Line Infantry Regiment, 1812

The one represented here is the uniform worn by the US regular infantry at the beginning of the war; clearly, this dress shows a strong British influence but has dark blue instead of red as main colour. This uniform was adopted since 1810, but only the seven regiments already existing before 1812 received it; the new ones, in fact, were given uniforms in different colours (due to the shortage of dark blue cloth). These "temporary" colours included black, dark grey, dark brown, white and light brown.

A2: Private, 5th Line Infantry Regiment, 1815

In 1813 the US regular infantry received the new uniform reproduced here, which looked quite simple if compared with the previous one issued in 1810: clearly the combat experiences of the first year of war had showed the importance of having a practical campaign dress. Also the shako was changed, being updated according to the latest British military fashions. The standard weapon of the US line infantry, represented here, was the M1795 Springfield musket.

A3: Sergeant, 22nd Line Infantry Regiment, 1813

This infantry regiment was one of those that made up the famous "Scott Brigade"; all the units that made up this brigade were dressed with a peculiar version of the M1813 uniform, having grey as main colour instead of dark blue (as usual, there was always shortage of the officially prescribed colour). The black embroidering on the chest, red waist-sash and sabre are all distinctive elements of sergeants.

A4: Private, 1st Rifle Regiment, 1814

The 1st Rifle Regiment had two different uniforms: one had a more conventional cut, being quite similar to the M1810 dress for the line infantry but having dark green as main colour instead of dark blue. The second uniform was the one represented here, used on campaign and consisting of a dark green "hunting shirt". The latter was the main item of dress worn by American settlers and militiamen. Since dark green cloth was quite rare, the three new regiments of rifles formed during the war were supplied with simple grey uniforms (very similar to those worn by the "Scott Brigade"). The weapon is an excellent M1803 Harpers Ferry rifled carbine.

A5: Private, Marines, 1812

The Marines adopted the uniform represented here since 1810; this was quite similar to those worn by the line infantry and 1st Rifle Regiment except for the yellow braiding on the chest. While line and light infantry officers wore shakos like their men, the officers of the Marine Corps had a black bicorn like the naval officers of the US Navy.

B1   **B2**   **B3**   **B4**   **B5**

Plate B: US Cavalry, Rangers and Technical Corps

B1: Matross, 2nd Artillery Regiment, 1812
In 1810 the foot artillery received the uniform represented here; this was quite similar to that worn by the regular infantry but since also the Royal Artillery was dressed in dark blue it looked very similar also the standard uniform of the British Artillery. In 1814 all the regiments of foot artillery were assembled into a single "Corps of Artillery" and received a new dress (much simpler than the one showed here): this new uniform was very similar to the M1813 dress for the line infantry.

B2: Sergeant, Light Artillery Regiment, 1812
Since the Light Artillery Regiment was a unit of mounted artillery, it had a dark blue uniform that was very similar to the one worn by the Light Dragoons (with three rows of buttons on the chest). In 1813 members of this regiment substituted their previous shako (reproduced here) with the new one adopted by the US Army in that year (compare with figure A2). Trumpeters of this unit, like in the cavalry regiments of the time, were distinguished by the fact of having a uniform in a distinctive colour (red in this case).

B3: Private, 1st Regiment of Light Dragoons, 1814
The dark blue uniform of the US Light Dragoons was extremely elegant, especially due to the presence of the ornate M1812 helmet (which showed a clear neo-classical influence). The latter was much more modern than the "Tarleton" helmets employed by most of the militia's light dragoons (who still wore uniforms inspired by Washington's Continental Army). When serving on horse the light dragoons had sabre and a couple of pistols; when on foot, the latters were replaced by an infantry musket.

B4: Sergeant, US Rangers, 1812
The Rangers of the regular army had no uniform and were dressed with their civilian clothing. This generally included "hunting shirts" like the one reproduced here and black slouch hats. Most of the non-uniformed militiamen from the various states, especially those coming from frontier areas, were generally equipped as the Ranger shown here. The only proper "military" element of his dress is the red waist-sash (showing that he is a sergeant).

B5: Master Workman, Corps of Artificers, 1814
The Corps of Artificers had the dark green uniform represented here, while the few officers of the Engineer Corps wore a dark blue dress with black facings and black bicorn as headgear. The Company of Sappers, Miners and Bombardiers was dressed quite similarly to the "Corps of Artillery" of 1814, but with yellow embroidering on the chest and black facings. The "Sea Fencibles" had not a "regular" uniform but most of them were dressed like sailors of the US Navy (with black round hat and dark blue jacket having multiple rows of buttons on the front).

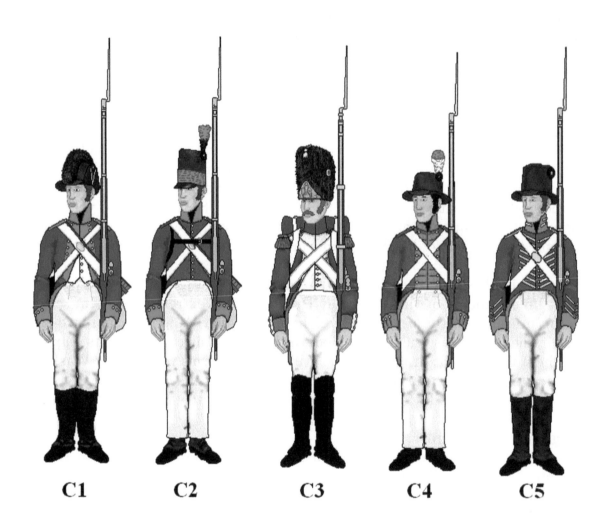

C1   C2   C3   C4   C5

Plate C: US State Militia, Part I

C1: Line infantryman, District of Columbia Militia, 1812
This was the uniform worn by the infantrymen of the District of Columbia Militia; officers had this same dress but with bicorn as headgear. The artillery also had this same uniform, but with black bicorn and with a red frontal plastron on the chest instead of simple red lapels. The light dragoons from the "1st Militia Legion of Washington" were dressed similarly to their equivalents of the regular army but with "Tarleton" helmets; those from the "2nd Militia Legion of Alexandria" were dressed in black coats and had "Tarleton" helmets.

C2: Line infantryman, Maryland Militia, 1814
The infantrymen of Maryland Militia had this simple campaign dress, which was quite similar to that adopted in 1813 by the regular infantry (excepting for the black shako with red band). Flank companies were distinguished by the following elements: white braiding on the collar, white shoulder wings, white frontal lapels of the coat, white cuffs piped in red and light blue band around the shako. Officers of all infantry companies wore the same shakos of the regulars.

C3: Grenadier, "Battalion of Orleans Volunteers" of the Louisiana Militia, 1815
The militiamen of New Orleans were mostly Francophone settlers, who generally wanted to preserve their French military traditions: this was particularly apparent in the uniforms worn by some companies of the "Battalion of Orleans Volunteers". The "Grenadiers Company", shown here, used a perfect copy of Napoleon's Imperial Guard Grenadiers uniform; officers of this company had golden gorgets and epaulettes in addition to their black bicorns (in perfect French style). Other Francophone units had uniforms copied from the contemporary French Army: the "Cannoniers-Bombardiers", for example, wore a uniform very similar to the one reproduced here but with red cords on the bearskin and dark blue trousers. The "Louisiana Blues", the only Anglophone company of the "Battalion of Orleans Volunteers", were dressed in the usual dark blue "hunting shirts" and black round hats.

C4: Line infantryman, New York Militia, 1812
The one shown here was the standard uniform of the New York Militia's line infantry; the artillery wore a very similar one but having a black bicorn as headgear. The cavalry, instead, wore red coats with black frontal plastron and facings (including collar, cuffs and shoulder wings). The headgear was a black "Tarleton" helmet. Some of the light dragoon regiments, however, were dressed in dark blue with frontal plastron and facings in red. The "Governor's Guard Battalion" was dressed exactly like the artillery, excepting for the band which members had red uniforms with Polish "czapka's".

C5: Line infantryman, Ohio Militia, 1814
Most of the Ohio militiamen, like in many frontier states and territories, wore no regular uniforms and were instead dressed in their civilian "hunting shirts". The proper uniform reproduced here was gradually adopted only during the course of the war.

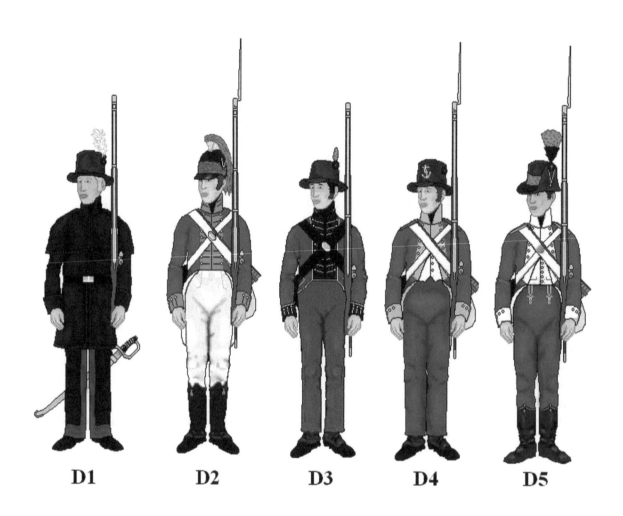

D1   **D2**   **D3**   **D4**   **D5**

Plate D: US State Militia, Part II

D1: Mounted rifleman, "Regiment of Mounted Volunteers" of the Kentucky Militia, 1813

The militia of Kentucky was almost entirely dressed in civilian clothing, like the one worn by the figure represented here. The "Regiment of Mounted Volunteers" that fought with great distinction at the River Raisin had black round hats and black "hunting shirts" with red fringes. Most of the Kentucky militiamen were armed with rifled muskets or carbines and had very comfortable moccasins.

D2: Light infantryman, Massachusetts Militia, 1812

The line infantry of Massachusetts Militia wore a uniform very similar to the one shown here, but with a black round hat as headgear instead of the helmet. In addition, the dark blue coat had red shoulder straps and red lapels on the front (instead of the plastron). The famous "Ancient and Honourable Artillery Company" had the same uniform reproduced here, but with a black bicorn with black plume as headgear. The "Company of Independent Boston Fusiliers", instead, had black bearskin and a red coat with dark blue facings. The "Boston Independent Cadets" had black bicorn and white coat with red frontal plastron and facings. The frontal plastron had yellow embroidering.

D3: Rifleman, "Trojan Greens Rifle Company" of the New York Militia, 1812

The dress shown here is a good example of the uniforms worn by the rifle units of the New York Militia; generally, these were dark green with black facings and could comprise different models of headgear. Light infantry units, instead, were usually dressed quite similarly to the line infantry but had a different headgear (which could be a leather helmet, in many cases copied from the light infantry dress of the Continental Army).

D4: Light infantryman, 2nd Brigade (Providence County) of the Rhode Island Militia, 1814

The light infantry of Rhode Island Militia had black round hats with a peculiar badge on the front: the latter reproduced an anchor, the main symbol of Rhode Island State. The "Providence Marine Corps of Artillery" had a uniform very similar to the one shown here, but with dark blue frontal lapels and facings piped in gold. Artillery companies had the same uniform represented here, but with red facings instead of yellow ones; headgear could be a round hat or a bicorn.

D5: Light infantryman, Virginia Militia, 1812

Most of the militiamen from Virginia were dressed quite simply, with "hunting shirts": these were dark blue with red fringes for the line infantrymen and red with dark red fringes for the riflemen. Headgear of the line infantrymen was the same reproduced in this figure, while the riflemen had no plume and wrapped band. The artillery, instead, was dressed as follows: black bicorn, dark blue coat with red lapels and facings, dark blue trousers and black boots.

E1   E2   E3   E4   E5

Plate E: US State Militia, Part III

E1: Trooper, "Charleston Light Dragoons" of the South Carolina Militia, 1812
The infantry from South Carolina Militia was dressed quite simply: black round hat with small dark blue plume, dark blue jacket with white piping and embroidering to collar, dark blue trousers. The artillery, instead, had a different dress that was much more similar to that worn by the light dragoons: black bicorn with red plume, dark blue coat with red frontal plastron and facings, white trousers and black gaiters.

E2: Light dragoon, Indiana Militia, 1812
Most of the Indiana militiamen, both on foot and mounted, were dressed in "hunting shirts" and thus had no proper uniforms. With the progression of time, however, the cavalry adopted the simple uniform shown here and the infantry started to be uniformed in black round hats and dark blue "hunting shirts" with white fringes.

E3: Trooper, "Barnard Troop of Light Cavalry" of the Vermont Militia, 1812
The foot militiamen of Vermont Militia were generally dressed in their civilian clothes, which frequently included a black round hat; the riflemen, instead, wore black round hats and white "hunting shirts" with green fringes. The artillery wore the following uniform: black bicorn, dark blue coat with red lapels and facings, dark blue trousers and black boots.

E4: Light dragoon, Norfolk County of the Virginia Militia, 1812
The cavalry of Virginia Militia was dressed in a peculiar green uniform, having "Tarleton" helmet as headgear. This kind of uniform had been adopted by North American cavalry since the days of the French-Indian War and American Revolution.

E5: Trooper, "Boston Hussars" of the Massachusetts Militia, 1812
The "Boston Hussars" were one of the most famous units of Massachusetts Militia, being uniformed in perfect European style with "dolman" and "pelisse" (the two main components of the standard hussar uniform). This corps was the only "hussar" unit of the US military forces during the War of 1812 against Britain.

F1   **F2**   **F3**   **F4**   **F5**

Plate F: British Regular Units

F1: Private, 1ˢᵗ Regiment of Foot ("Royal Scots"), 1813

The one represented here was the basic uniform worn by the British line and light infantry, the different regiments being distinguished by distinctive facing colours (dark blue in this case). Trousers were dark grey during winter and white during summer. The plume on the shako was half white and half red for fusiliers, entirely white for grenadiers and entirely green for light infantrymen. The 10th "Royal Veteran Battalion" was dressed quite similarly to the unit shown here, with dark blue as distinctive facing colour. The "Fencibles" units were uniformed like the line infantry. The regiments of light infantry obviously had green plumes on the shakos for all their companies. The fusilier companies of the line infantry had normal shoulder straps, while the grenadier and light infantry ones had shoulder wings. The regiments of light infantry had shoulder wings for all their companies. Line infantry regiments were armed with the "heavy" version of the Brown Bess musket, while the light infantry ones had a "light" version of the same musket.

F2: Private, 93ʳᵈ Regiment of Foot ("Sutherland Highlanders"), 1815

The Scottish regiments of infantry were dressed like the British ones, but wore distinctive headgear and traditional "kilt"; in this case the hat is of the famous "Balmoral" type and the "kilt" has been replaced by "trews" (trousers made with the same "tartan" cloth of the "kilts"). Each Scottish regiment had a different kind of "tartan", which was a symbol of its past history.

F3: Rifleman, 60ᵗʰ Regiment of Foot ("Royal American"), 1814

The riflemen of the 60th Regiment of Foot were dressed in dark green but had distinctive dark blue trousers; the riflemen of the 95th Regiment of Foot, instead, had dark green trousers. Most of the Canadian light infantry units formed during the war, being influenced by the uniforms of the regular "Rifles", adopted green as main colour for their uniforms and had three frontal rows of buttons on their jackets. The standard weapon of the British riflemen was the excellent Baker carbine.

F4: Private, 19ᵗʰ Regiment of Light Dragoons, 1814

The 19th Regiment of Light Dragoons wore the uniform adopted in 1812 by the British light cavalry, which included a shako as headgear. The distinctive colour of this unit was yellow; the 14th Regiment of Light Dragoons, instead, had orange as facing colour. The "Inniskilling" Dragoons were a unit of heavy cavalry and thus wore a different uniform with black helmet and red jacket. The Royal Artillery was dressed in dark blue, quite similarly to the foot artillery of the US Army; the Royal Engineers, instead, were dressed like the artillery but with red as main colour.

F5: Private, 5th "West India" Regiment, 1812

The infantry regiments formed with black soldiers of the West Indies were dressed in this peculiar uniform, having frontal plastron and facings in distinctive colour. The 1st Regiment had white as facing colour, while the 2nd Regiment had yellow frontal plastron and facings. Officers and NCOs of these regiments wore the same standard uniform of British line infantry units, respectively with round hat and shako as headgears. The Swiss regiments were uniformed exactly like all the other British line infantry units: "De Watteville" Regiment had medium blue as distinctive colour; "De Meuron" Regiment had black. The Royal Marines were dressed like the line infantry, but with black round hats and dark blue as facing colour; the "Colonial Marines", instead, wore the following: black round hat, white jacket with dark blue facings and white trousers.

G1　　　**G2**　　　**G3**　　　**G4**　　　**G5**

Plate G: Canadian Militia and Volunteers, Part I

G1: Militiaman, "Sedentary Militia" of Upper Canada, 1813

The "Sedentary Militia" of Upper Canada generally wore no proper uniforms: this is the case of the militiaman reproduced here, who is a Scottish settler coming from the Dundas County or Glengarry County (which were mostly inhabited by Scots). The ethnic origin of this militiaman is clearly shown by his headgear, "kilt" and socks. The white armband, worn by members of the "Sedentary Militia", was the only element of their dress that distinguished them from civilians. As the war progressed, a certain number of the "sedentary" militiamen started to wear red or dark green jackets like those of the British regulars or "Embodied" militiamen. Officers of the "Sedentary Militia" had red uniforms with black round hats, like their colleagues of Lower Canada.

G2: Private, "Select Embodied Militia" of Upper Canada, 1813

This was the uniform worn by the single battalion of "Select Embodied Militia" raised in Upper Canada, having dark green as main colour. The "Glengarry Light Infantry" was dressed exactly like the regulars of the 95th Regiment of Foot, with dark green or grey trousers. The "Caldwell's Rangers" were uniformed more or less in the same way, but with grey trousers instead of dark green ones.

G3: Militiaman, "Sedentary Militia" of Nova Scotia, 1813

This uniform was worn by the "Sedentary Militia" of Nova Scotia; the "activated" militiamen of the colony, instead, were dressed as the normal British line infantry (with medium blue as distinctive colour). The "activated" riflemen, instead, were dressed more or less like figure F3. The militiamen of New Brunswick were dressed like British line infantrymen, but some companies had black round hats instead of shakos. The "Saint John's Volunteer Rangers" of Newfoundland were dressed like figure F3, while the militiamen of Cape Breton Island were dressed exactly like the "Sedentary Militia" of Nova Scotia. The militiamen of Prince Edward Island were dressed quite similarly to the figure shown here, but with red jackets having dark blue facings.

G4: Private, 2nd Battalion of Montréal "Urban Militia", 1813

This was the uniform worn by the 2nd and 3rd Battalions of Montréal's urban militia; the 1st Battalion, instead, was dressed quite similarly to figure G3. Flank companies of the 2nd and 3rd Battalions had white trousers instead of dark blue ones. Clearly the Francophone and Anglophone units had different uniforms, in order to underline their ethnic origin.

G5: Private, Battalion of Trois-Rivières "Urban Militia", 1813

This uniform with black round hat was worn by the single infantry battalion of Trois-Rivières' urban militia. The battalions from Québec City, instead, were dressed like the British line infantry albeit with distinctive facing colours for each of the three battalions. The "Québec Volunteers" were uniformed like the British line infantry but had black round hats.

H1 **H2** **H3** **H4** **H5**

Plate H: Canadian militias and volunteers, part II

H1: Soldier, "Corps of Canadian Voyageurs" (Lower Canada), 1812

Both the "Corps of Canadian Voyageurs" and the "Provincial Commissariat Voyageurs" of Lower Canada wore no regular uniforms but were dressed with their own civilian clothing. This figure shows a "voyageur" with his winter dress and equipment, which enabled him to survive in the woods also with extremely cold temperatures. Most of the "voyageurs" were hunters and thus their main weapon was a rifled musket. Like in Upper Canada, the "Sedentary Militia" of Lower Canada wore no proper uniform: its members were mostly dressed like the figure reproduced here, with fur caps and great-coats. Only officers had uniforms, which were very similar to those of their British line infantry equivalents excepting for the headgear (which was a black round hat).

H2: Soldier, "Frontier Light Infantry" (Lower Canada), 1813

This kind of grey uniform, quite simple and easy to produce, was extremely popular among Canadian light infantry units. It was worn also by the "Independent Company of Militia Volunteers", as well as by the "Canadian Chasseurs" (albeit the latter had black shakos and three rows of buttons on the front of the jacket).

H3: Officer, "Canadian Voltiguers" (Lower Canada), 1812

The officers of the "Canadian Voltiguers" were dressed like the one represented here, with a uniform that was extremely similar to that worn by their equivalents of the regular 95th Regiment of Foot (excepting for the headgear, which was a black bearskin). The soldiers of the "Canadian Voltiguers", instead, were uniformed exactly like figure H2.

H4: Officer, 2nd "Leeds Rifle Company" (Upper Canada), 1812

The "Volunteers of 1812", raised in Upper Canada, wore different uniforms according to their county of origin: the rifle company from Leeds County represented here had a very elegant dress, while those coming from Glengarry County had more or less the same uniform of figure F2 but with dark green coats.

H5: Trooper, "Canadian Light Dragoons" (Lower Canada), 1813

This simple uniform with "Tarleton" helmet, inspired by the old dress of the British regular light cavalry, was worn also by the "Provincial Light Dragoons" of Upper Canada. The "Compagnie des Guides", instead, wore a much simpler uniform consisting of entirely dark grey jacket and trousers; troopers had black round hat as headgear, while officers had "Tarleton" helmets. The "Dorchester Provincial Light Dragoons" were dressed similarly to the figure shown here, but their "Tarleton" helmets had brown fur and no red band wrapped around them. The cavalry from Québec urban militia was dressed like the "Canadian Light Dragoons" but with additional white braiding (on collar and cuffs) and with white frogging on the chest. The cavalry from Montréal urban militia was dressed like the regular light dragoons (see figure F4) but with red facing colour. The "Royal Militia Artillery" of Lower Canada and the "Incorporated Artillery

Company" of Upper Canada were dressed like the Royal Artillery; the "Corps of Provincial Royal Artillery Drivers" of Lower Canada, the "Provincial Royal Artillery Drivers" of Upper Canada and the "Corps of Provincial Artificers" of Upper Canada were all uniformed like their British regular equivalents.

Select Bibliography

Stuart Asquith, *The War of 1812: A Campaign Guide to the War with America*, Partizan Press, 2008

Carl Benn, *The War of 1812*, Osprey Publishing, 2002

René Chartrand, *Canadian Military Heritage:* Volume II (1755-1871), Art Global, 1995

René Chartrand, *British forces in North America 1793-1815*, Osprey Publishing, 1998

René Chartrand, *A Most Warlike Appearance: Uniforms, Flags and Equipment of the United States in the War of 1812*, Ottawa, 2011

René Chartrand, *A Scarlet Coat: Uniforms, Flags and Equipment of British forces in the War of 1812*, Ottawa, 2011

Ed Gilbert, *Frontier Militiaman in the War of 1812*, Osprey Publishing, 2008

Michael G. Johnson, *American Woodland Indians*, Osprey Publishing, 1990

Philip Katcher, *The American War 1812-1814*, Osprey Publishing, 1990

James L. Kochan, *The United States Army 1812-1815*, Osprey Publishing, 2000

James L. Kochan, *The United States Army 1783-1811*, Osprey Publishing, 2001

John Latimer, *Niagara 1814,* Osprey Publishing, 2009

John R. Maas, *Defending a New Nation: 1783-1811*, Center of Military History of the US Army, 2013

Olivier Millet, *Les Armées de la Guerre de 1812*, Web published, 2013

Tim Pickles, *New Orleans 1815*, Osprey Publishing, 1994

Francis P. Prucha, *Sword of the Republic: The United States Army on the Frontier 1783-1846*, Macmillan Press, 1968

Scott S. Sheads, *The Chesapeake Campaigns 1813-1815*, Osprey Publishing, 2014

The Company of Military Historians, *Military uniforms in America: years of growth 1796-1851*, Presidio Press, 1977

Russell F. Weigley, *History of the United States Army*, Macmillan Press, 1967

John F. Winkler, *Wabash 1791*, Osprey Publishing, 2011

John F. Winkler, *Fallen Timbers 1794*, Osprey Publishing, 2013

John F. Winkler, *Tippecanoe 1811*, Osprey Publishing, 2015

John F. Winkler, *The Thames 1813*, Osprey Publishing, 2016

INDEX

Look for more books from Winged Hussar Publishing, LLC – E-books, paperbacks and Limited Edition hardcovers. The best in history, science fiction and fantasy at:

https://www. wingedhussarpublishing.com
or follow us on Facebook at:
Winged Hussar Publishing LLC
Or on twitter at:
WingHusPubLLC

For information and upcoming publications

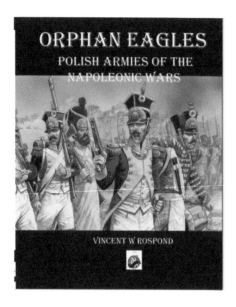

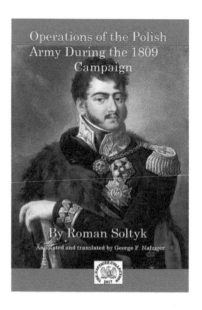

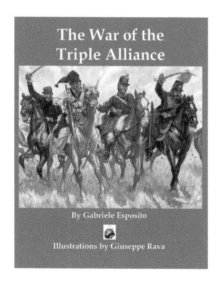

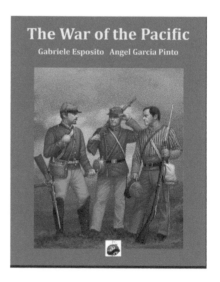

About the Author

Gabriele Esposito is a researcher of Contemporary History at the "Luigi Vanvitelli" University of Campania. Scholar of military history and uniformology with extensive international experience, for years he has worked as an author and freelance researcher with the most important publishers active in the field of history military. These include Osprey Publishing, Winged Hussar Publishing, Partizan Press and Pen and Sword. He writes regularly for the most important dedicated magazines in the world to military history.